Kinship Bere(

A Special Issue
of
OMEGA — Journal of Death and Dying

**Edited by
Brian de Vries**

BAYWOOD PUBLISHING COMPANY, INC.
AMITYVILLE, NEW YORK 11701

Copyright © 1997 by the Baywood Publishing Company, Inc., Amityville, New York. All rights reserved. Printed in the United States of America on acid-free recycled paper.

ISBN: 0-89503-182-5

TABLE OF CONTENTS

Introduction: Kinship Bereavement in Later Life
 Brian de Vries 1

Case Histories of Traumatic Grief
 *Holly G. Prigerson, M. Katherine Shear, Andrew J. Bierhals,
 Paul A. Pilkonis, Lee Wolfson, Martica Hall, Dianna L. Zonarich, and
 Charles F. Reynolds, III* 9

Sibling Bereavement in Late Life
 Judith C. Hays, Deborah T. Gold, and Carl F. Pieper 25

The Role of Gender in Middle-Age Children's Responses to Parent Death
 Miriam S. Moss, Nancy Resch, and Sidney Z. Moss 43

The Adult Child's Acceptance of Parent Death
 Anne R. Bower 67

Long-Term Psychological and Somatic Consequences of Later Life
 Parental Bereavement
 *Brian de Vries, Christopher G. Davis, Camille B. Wortman, and
 Darrin R. Lehman* 97

Grandparents' Reactions to the Death of a Grandchild:
 An Exploratory Factor Analytic Study
 P. S. Fry 119

Kinship Bereavement in Later Life: Understanding Variations in
 Cause, Course, and Consequence
 Brian de Vries 141

INTRODUCTION:
KINSHIP BEREAVEMENT IN LATER LIFE

BRIAN DE VRIES, PH.D.
University of British Columbia, and
San Francisco State University, California

ABSTRACT

This article introduces a volume devoted to the examination of later-life bereavement: an analysis of variation in cause, course, and consequence. Six articles address and represent this variation and comprise this volume: 1) Prigerson et al. present case histories of the traumatic grief of spouses; 2) Hays et al. highlight the bereavement experiences of siblings in contrast to those spouses and friends; 3) Moss et al. address the role of gender in middle-aged children's responses to parent death; 4) Bower focuses on the language adopted by these adult children in accepting the death of a parent; 5) de Vries et al. explore the long-term, longitudinal effects on the psychological and somatic functioning of parents following the death of an adult child; and 6) Fry presents the short-term and longitudinal reactions of grandparents to the death of a grandchild. A concluding article is offered by de Vries stressing both the unique and common features of these varied bereavement experiences touching on some of the empirical issues and suggesting potential implications and applications.

It has been estimated that in any given year, over eight million Americans of all ages will become bereft of an immediate family member [1]. Of course, at some point in time, individuals in all families will endure such a loss—an eventuality that increases dramatically with age. Kastenbaum [2], Lieberman [3], and others have commented that the impact of a death may be greater for survivors in later life than at other junctures of the life course. For example, the significant tests of time endured by long-standing relationships may lead to a melding of lives and more varied, broadly-based and richer memories [4], potentially complicating post-bereavement adjustment. Furthermore, later-life bereavement befalls individuals whose resources to cope with such stress may be already compromised or diminished through the repeated charges on health and well-being of a long life. The exponentially increasing numbers of older adults and the particular conditions and circumstances of their bereavement suggest that this is an important area of research with significant implications for practice. These are the thoughts that underlie this special issue of *Omega: Journal of Death and Dying* and the articles that follow.

BACKGROUND

Much of the current information on later-life bereavement derives from the relatively extensive literature on spousal loss [5, 6]. As Arbuckle and de Vries [7] have suggested, this level of attention to widowhood reflects both the demographics of American society and the prevalence of this age-graded, "most stressful life event" [8]: approximately 50 percent of all women and 12 percent of all men over the age of sixty-five have survived the death of their spouse [9]. Overall, the literature on widowhood has been more issue-driven than theory-driven [10] and empirical contributors have largely focused their efforts on the measurement of emotional distress. Typical reports detail higher levels of depression, stress, and dysphoria among those recently bereft of a spouse [11, 12] with effects generally returning to levels not significantly different from the non-bereaved beyond the first year post loss [13]. Similar patterns of initial assaults on functioning followed by its eventual restoration also have been reported using measures of life satisfaction [13], psychological symptoms [14], and self-perceived physical health [13, 15]. Findings such as these, in conjunction with both the prevailing cultural beliefs about the course of recovery from bereavement and the traditional models of dying, death, and loss [16-18], have furnished widespread assumptions that grieving individuals advance through variously defined stages or phases en route to recovery [19] within a relatively circumscribed period of time, often defined as a single year [20].

Recently, however, an increasing number of reports (including the articles of this volume) have either implicitly or explicitly questioned these assumptions. For example, the linearity inherent in a sequence of stages must now be reconciled with findings of overlapping and successive periods of anger, guilt, anxiety, and sadness [21] and even moments of pleasure, pride, and relief [11]; philosophical, spiritual, social, economic, and physiological realms of functioning are reportedly affected by loss [1]. The nature or essence of recovery has been questioned by Weiss [22] and others with evidence of bereavement effects enduring four years [23] and even up to fifteen years [7] following that death. Finally, and perhaps most germane to this special issue, several authors have cautioned that all family deaths are not equal [3]: a complete and thorough understanding of the course and substance of bereavement in later life requires an analysis of the many family deaths that may accompany older age.

For example, the death of a spouse signals a change in the present and daily conditions of one's life and in one's social relations. The death of a sibling alludes to one's own mortality and threatened history. The death of a parent similarly occasions a permanent break with connections to the past as middle-aged orphaned grievers enter the omega generation. The death of a child severs connections to the future and represents a violation of the natural order of the universe. The death of a grandchild and the concomitant generational extension exacerbates these reactions. Understanding both these variations and commonalities will add to our knowledge of both bereavement *and* the nature of family ties in old age; as noted by Deck and Folta [24], "the study of grief is more than the study of symptoms and possible pathology; it is the study of people and their most intimate relationships" [24, p. 80]. These remarks serve to introduce the broader context within which this compilation of articles is cast: a multi-method and multi-dimensional examination of bereavement in response to the variety of family losses that accompany the later years.

CONTENTS OF THIS SPECIAL ISSUE

This collection of articles is an outgrowth of the Death, Dying, Bereavement and Widowhood Interest Group of the Gerontological Society of America and comprises empirical accounts of several distinct family losses: the death of a spouse, sibling, parent, child, and grandchild. These articles represent normative and non-normative losses; the juxtaposition of short-term and long-term bereavement reactions; cross-sectional and longitudinal comparisons; sociological, psychological, and psycholinguistic research paradigms; national and regional level data; and qualitative and quantitative analytic strategies. The articles and their approaches are as diverse and varied as are the experiences they describe, yet each contributes something of value to the more singular and superordinate goal of understanding kinship bereavement in the later years.

Prigerson, Shear, Bierhals, Pilkonis, Wolfson, Hall, Zonarich, and Reynolds, the authors of the first article, describe the concepts of traumatic and anticipatory grief reflected in three case study illustrations of older spouses. They note that the symptoms of traumatic grief are distinct from those of bereavement-related depression and anxiety and are strikingly similar to symptoms of Posttraumatic Stress Disorder. Prigerson et al. propose a model, and give it texture through the case studies they present, hypothesizing causal links between childhood experiences (such as abuse or conflict), insecure or unstable attachment styles (including excessive dependency and defensive separation), personality traits (such as unstable self-image and affect), the loss of the relationship and traumatic symptomatology. This article neatly sets the stage for an analysis of variability and diversity in bereavement reactions, some of which have their origins in events, circumstances, cognition, and affect that predate the death.

The second article, by Hays, Gold, and Pieper, examines perhaps the most common *and* understudied form of later-life kinship bereavement—the death of a sibling—using the data of almost 3200 older bereaved adults interviewed as part of a multi-center epidemiological study. Hays et al. borrow from attachment theory (similar to Prigerson et al.), the writings of Weiss as well as the literature on coping, particularly noting the significance of the appraisal of the loss, to explore how reactions to the death of a sibling are similar to and different from the death of a spouse or the death of a friend. Bereaved siblings suffer greater functional, cognitive and subjective health deficits than do those bereft of a spouse or friend, although the spousally bereft suffered more from mood alterations and social support deficits. Subtle and intriguing differences emerge in responses to the death of a sister versus a brother suggestive of a more complex role for gender than is typically engaged in bereavement research.

The third and fourth article by Moss, Resch, and Moss and by Bower, respectively, discuss the surprisingly little studied but normative phenomenon of bereavement associated with the death of an (elderly) parent. Moss et al. explore in detail some of the complex effects of gender (of parent, of child, and of the parent-child dyad), suggested above, with extensive questionnaire data from over 200 middle-aged children. They report major differences between sons and daughters, partially attributable to traditional gender roles, with daughters of deceased fathers revealing a distinctive pattern of results. Several other characteristics of the parent and child were associated with variations in bereavement outcomes: the context of the parent's final year of life; the age and socioeconomic status of the child; personality characteristics of the child including a sense of mastery and feelings of guilt; as well as the overall quality of the parent-child relationship.

Bower presents a qualitative analysis of the language used by fifty of these adult children in their accounts of acceptance of parental death. The analysis of these in-depth interview transcripts provide an unique perspective into both the content and the construct of death acceptance, a term frequently used but rarely defined in the bereavement literature. Bower finds that the vast majority of respondents report that they have accepted the death and explain their responses in ways that juxtapose the more cognitive activity of acceptance with their strong emotional reactions to the loss. Themes of acceptance followed from values and beliefs about the nature of death (e.g., as a fact, as an endpoint, as God's will, or as part of the natural order of the universe) in association with powerful feelings and memories. Non-acceptance themes concerned maintaining interactions, unresolved problems or the unacceptability of death.

de Vries, Davis, Wortman, and Lehman author the fifth article and address a loss that is said to violate the natural order of the universe: the death of an adult child. de Vries et al. draw their sample of over 1000 respondents, seventy-seven of whom are bereft of a child, from a longitudinal data set of randomly sampled adults who responded to questions on health, stress, and productivity. They make special reference to the personal and socio-demographic context in which bereavement and adaptation occurs, reporting both subtle effects (i.e., variations in *sources* of life satisfaction and worry), as well as effects of over ten years in duration (e.g., elevated levels of depression and accelerated deterioration of health). These long-term effects represent some of the extreme anguish felt by older parents about a loss that challenges life's meaning and purpose.

Many of the reactions to the untimely death of a young person as reported by parents are mirrored in the responses of grandparents. This is the topic addressed by Fry in her qualitative and quantitative analysis of over 150 bereaved grandparents, a small subsample of whom participated in a six month follow-up. Fry describes six factors that characterize the grief reactions of grandparents: a feeling of emotional rupturing; survivor guilt; regrets about relationships with the deceased child; a need to restructure relationships with family members and living grandchildren; concomitant anxieties; and, the process of recovery. Additionally, she presents grandparents' accounts of a shattering of one's groundedness in the world and the pain they feel for the adult child (i.e., the grieving parent). These elder watchdogs of the family experience bereavement from multiple perspectives [25].

The important and overarching theme underscored by these articles is the diverse experience of bereavement in later life—a diversity of cause, course, and consequence. The bereavement may be occasioned by family deaths spanning several generations, take a number of forms and manifest itself in a variety of ways over varying periods of time. The after-image of these reports, however, is not one of unpredictable chaos or idiosyncrasy; rather it is one of complexity and relational specificity; of attention to context; of sensitivity to relationship roles and nature; and of fluid trajectories. de Vries summarizes the central (unique and common) findings of these articles offering thoughts to help integrate this diversity and complexity in the service of a more complete understanding of later life kinship bereavement.

REFERENCES

1. M. Osterweis, F. Solomon, and M. Green, *Bereavement: Reactions, Consequences and Care*, National Academy Press, Washington, D.C., 1984.
2. R. Kastenbaum, Dying and Death: A Life-Span Approach, in *Handbook of the Psychology of Aging* (2nd Edition), J. E. Birren and K. W. Schaie (eds.), Van Nostrand Reinhold, New York, pp. 619-643, 1985.
3. M. A. Lieberman, All Family Losses are Not Equal, *Journal of Family Psychology*, 2, pp. 368-372, 1989.
4. P. C. Rosenblatt, Grief: The Social Context of Private Feelings, in *Handbook of Bereavement: Theory, Research, and Interventions*, M. S. Stroebe, W. Stroebe, and R. O. Hansson (eds.), Cambridge University Press, New York, pp. 102-111, 1993.

5. I. Levav, Mortality and Psychopathology Following the Death of an Adult Child: An Epidemiological Review, *Israel Journal of Psychiatry Related Sciences, 19*, pp. 23-28, 1982.
6. M. S. Moss, E. L. Lesher, and S. Z. Moss, Impact of the Death of an Adult Child on Elderly Parents: Some Observations, *Omega: Journal of Death and Dying, 17*, pp. 209-218, 1986-87.
7. N. W. Arbuckle and B. de Vries, The Long-Term Effects of Later Life Spousal and Parental Bereavement on Personal Functioning, *The Gerontologist, 35*:5, pp. 637-647, 1995.
8. R. H. Holmes and R. H. Rahe, The Social Readjustment Rating Scale, *Journal of Psychosomatic Research, 11*, pp. 213-218, 1967.
9. M. S. Stroebe, W. Stroebe, and R. O. Hansson, Bereavement Research: An Historical Introduction, *Journal of Social Issues, 44*:3, pp. 1-18, 1988.
10. W. Stroebe and M. S. Stroebe, *Bereavement and Health*, Cambridge University Press, New York, 1987.
11. M. Caserta and D. A. Lund, Bereavement Stress and Coping Among Older Adults: Expectations versus the Actual Experience, *Omega: Journal of Death and Dying, 25*, pp. 33-45, 1992.
12. J. N. Breckenridge, D. Gallagher, L. W. Thompson, and J. Peterson, Characteristic Depressive Symptoms of Bereaved Elders, *Journal of Gerontology, 41*, pp. 163-168, 1986.
13. D. A. Lund, M. S. Caserta, and M. F. Dimond, Impact of Spousal Bereavement on the Subjective Well-Being of Older Adults, in *Older Bereaved Spouses: Research with Practical Applications*, D. A. Lund (ed.), Hemisphere, New York, 1989.
14. L. W. Thompson, D. Gallagher-Thompson, A. Futterman, M. Gilewski, and J. Peterson, The Effects of Later-Life Spousal Bereavement Over a 30-Month Interval, *Psychology and Aging, 6*, pp. 434-441, 1991.
15. R. R. McCrae and P. R. Costa, Psychological Resilience among Widowed Men and Women: A 10-Year Follow-Up of a National Sample, *Journal of Social Issues, 44*:3, pp. 129-142, 1988.
16. J. Bowlby, *Attachment and Loss (Vol. 3): Loss: Sadness and Depression*, Hogarth Press, London, 1980.
17. E. Kübler-Ross, *Death: The Final Stage of Growth*, Prentice-Hall, Englewood Cliffs, New Jersey, 1975.
18. J. Worden, *Grief Counseling and Grief Therapy*, Springer, New York, 1982.
19. T. A. Rando, Parental Bereavement: An Exception to the General Conceptualizations of Mourning, in *Parental Loss of a Child*, T. A. Rando (ed.), Research Press, Champaign, Illinois, 1986.
20. M. S. Stroebe, R. O. Hansson, and W. Stroebe, Contemporary Themes and Controversies in Bereavement Research, in *Handbook of Bereavement: Theory, Research, and Intervention*, M. S. Stroebe, W. Stroebe, and R. O. Hansson (eds.), Cambridge University Press, New York, pp. 457-475, 1993.
21. J. R. Averill and E. P. Nunley, Grief As An Emotion and As a Disease: A Social-Constructionist Perspective in *Handbook of Bereavement: Theory, Research, and Intervention*, M. S. Stroebe, W. Stroebe, and R. O. Hansson (eds.), Cambridge University Press, New York, pp. 77-90, 1993.

22. R. S. Weiss, Loss and Recovery, in *Handbook of Bereavement: Theory, Research, and Intervention*, M. S. Stroebe, W. Stroebe, and R. O. Hansson (eds.), Cambridge University Press, New York, pp. 271-284, 1993.
23. D. R. Lehman, C. B. Wortman, and A. Williams, Long-Term Effects of Losing a Spouse or Child in a Motor Vehicle Crash, *Journal of Personality and Social Psychology, 52*, pp. 218-231, 1987.
24. E. S. Deck and J. R. Folta, The Friend-Griever, in *Disenfranchised Grief: Recognizing Hidden Sorrow*, K. J. Doka (ed.), Lexington Books, Lexington, Massachusetts, pp. 77-89, 1989.
25. L. E. Troll, Grandparents: The Family Watchdogs, in *Family Relationships in Later Life*, T. Brubaker (ed.), Sage Publications, Newbury Park, California, pp. 63-74, 1983.

CASE HISTORIES OF TRAUMATIC GRIEF*

HOLLY G. PRIGERSON, PH.D.	LEE WOLFSON, M.ED.
M. KATHERINE SHEAR, M.D.	MARTICA HALL, PH.D.
ANDREW J. BIERHALS, B.S.	DIANNA L. ZONARICH, B.S.
PAUL A. PILKONIS, PH.D.	CHARLES F. REYNOLDS, III, M.D.

*University of Pittsburgh School of Medicine,
Western Psychiatric Institute and Clinic*

ABSTRACT

The symptoms of traumatic grief have been shown to be distinct from those of bereavement-related depression and anxiety among elderly widows and widowers, and bare striking resemblance to symptoms of Posttraumatic Stress Disorder (PTSD). In light of the findings demonstrating that traumatic grief is associated with a heightened risk of critical mental and physical health outcomes, it is important to understand the underlying mechanisms that may put bereaved individuals at risk of developing traumatic grief. Attachment theory offers an explanation for why loss of a stabilizing relationship might be traumatic for individuals who possess insecure or unstable attachments (e.g., excessive dependency, defensive separation, compulsive caregiving) and self-regulatory deficits (e.g., identity disturbances, difficulty with affect modulation). A model illustrating hypothesized causal linkages between childhood experiences, attachment and personality traits, dissolution of a stabilizing relationship, and traumatic symptomatology is proposed. Case histories of late-life pre- and post-loss traumatic grievers are presented and discussed in terms of their compatibility with the proposed model.

*Supported by MH01100, MH37869, MH43832, MH00295, MH30915, MH32260, and MH52247.

Recent research challenges conventional notions of what constitute the emotional complications of bereavement. In contrast with the *DSM-IV* [1] which considers the symptoms of a Major Depressive Episode as the only treatment-worthy complication of bereavement, the results of two recent studies [2, 3] reveal that certain symptoms of traumatic grief (e.g., yearning, searching, preoccupation with thoughts of the deceased, avoidance of reminders of the deceased) are distinct from the symptoms of bereavement-related depression (e.g., worthlessness, psychomotor retardation, apathy, low self-esteem, sad mood) and anxiety (e.g., feeling tense, dread, nervous, sweating, palpitations).

Not only have the symptoms traumatic grief been shown to form a symptom profile distinct from that of bereavement-related depression and anxiety in late life, but the symptoms of traumatic grief assessed at baseline (3 months post-loss) were found to predict impaired global functioning, poor sleep, sad mood, and low self-esteem at eighteen months post-loss [2]. In another study of spousally bereaved elders, symptoms of traumatic grief assessed at approximately six months post-loss were found to predict both traumatic grief and depressive symptomatology at twelve and eighteen months post-loss [3]. A recent report reveals that symptoms of traumatic grief assessed at approximately six months post-loss predict such critical health outcomes as incidence of cancer, high blood pressure, cardiac events, increased consumption of alcohol and tobacco, and suicidal ideation one-to-two years post-loss [4].

Some preliminary evidence suggests that the symptoms of post-loss "traumatic" grief are virtually identical to the symptoms of pre-loss "anticipatory" grief [5]. For example, bereaved individuals who possess the traumatic grief symptoms of yearning or longing for the deceased, preoccupation with thoughts of the deceased to the point of impaired daily functioning, feeling disbelief and stunned by the death, avoidance of reminders of the deceased, auditory and visual hallucinations of the deceased, pain in the same parts of the body as that experienced by the spouse prior to his/her death, bitterness and survivor guilt concerning the death, are the same people who report these very symptoms prior to the death (e.g., yearning for the spouse to be as s/he once was, preoccupation with thoughts about the dying spouse, bitterness over the impending death of the spouse). Not only do the total scores for anticipatory and traumatic grief tend to be quite similar (e.g., those in the "syndromal" range of anticipatory grief tend to be the same individuals who are in the "syndromal" range of traumatic grief), but the relative severity of particular symptoms also appear to remain stable pre-to-post-loss (e.g., those who "always" are preoccupied with thoughts of the dying spouse and who "never" feel bitter over the impending death of their spouse appear to be the same individuals who report that they are "always" preoccupied with thoughts of their deceased spouse and are "never" bitter over the his/her death). This suggests that these pathological grief reactions may have more to do with an individual's enduring personality characteristics than with characteristics of the death.

Although our earlier results had identified eight traumatic grief symptoms that predicted future impairments secondary to bereavement (i.e., yearning, preoccupation with thoughts of the deceased, crying, searching for the deceased, disbelief about the death, being stunned by the death, acceptance of the death) [2], we sought to develop a scale that would encompass a broader, yet more specific, range of traumatic grief symptoms. Whereas extant scales of grief measure symptoms of grief in general (i.e., both normal and pathological), they do not focus exclusively on the symptoms of grief that are particularly maladaptive. As a consequence, scales such as the Texas Revised Inventory of Grief (TRIG: 6) are over inclusive with respect to traumatic grief.

For example, the Texas Revised Inventory of Grief (TRIG) includes benign symptoms of grief such as "No one will ever take the place in my life of the person who died" and "Things and people around me still remind me of the person who died" which would not be expected to be associated with maladaptation to the loss. The TRIG asks the respondent about crying in three separate statements, which seems redundant for the isolation of a unique set of indicators of traumatic grief. In addition, the Grief Measurement Scale (GMS: 7) includes symptoms associated with anxiety disorders, such as the statements concerning a dread of impending doom, fear of losing control of one's feelings, and feeling tense, nervous, and fidgety. Furthermore, the GMS contains depressive items (the Center for Epidemiological Studies-Depression subscale) as one of its three subcategories of symptoms. In these ways, the most prominent grief scales appear to contain superfluous items for the assessment of traumatic grief and may also confound assessment of traumatic grief by including measures of general grief, depression, and anxiety.

At the same time, extant grief scales may also be under inclusive with respect to symptoms of traumatic grief. Scales such as the TRIG and GMS omit many of the most potentially threatening symptoms of grief. Symptoms such as survivor guilt, bitterness over the death, jealousy of others who have not experienced a similar loss, distraction to the point of disruption in the performance of one's normal activities, and lack of trust in others as a consequence of the loss have not been assessed in existing scales of grief. The TRIG also does not include auditory and visual hallucinations, and neither the TRIG nor the GMS contain an item to assess pain in the same parts of the body as that experienced by the deceased (i.e., the so-called "identification" symptoms of grief-related facsimile illness). These foreboding grief-related symptoms appear to be more likely to reflect greater difficulty accepting the death.

The Inventory of Complicated Grief was developed to provide a reliable and valid assessment of all the symptoms of grief that we expected to be particularly maladaptive. The Inventory of Complicated Grief (ICG; 8), which omitted the depressive and anxiety-related symptoms and focused on the more pathological symptoms of grief, has been shown to provide a reliable and valid assessment. Not only were respondents who had ICG scores in the upper 20th percentile significantly more impaired on virtually all assessed quality of life domains than those below that threshold, but they were significantly more impaired that respondents in the upper 20th percentile of the TRIG. Upon examination of the items that seemed to best characterize traumatic grief, it appeared that the core traumatic grief symptoms (e.g., intrusive thoughts, avoidance behaviors, survivor guilt) overlapped extensively with the symptoms of Posttraumatic Stress Disorder (PTSD). We decided to examine more explicitly the extent to which symptoms of traumatic grief would meet *DSM-IV* [1] criteria for PTSD.

With respect to meeting *DSM-IV* [1] PTSD criteria, we are in the process of preparing a report in which we describe the following results: Aside from meeting the *DSM-IV* section A.1 criterion for PTSD (i.e., traumatic grief symptoms occur secondary to the actual or threatened death or serious injury to self or significant other), traumatic grievers also meet the section A.2 criterion that the event evokes intense fear, helplessness, or horror. Our construct of traumatic grief includes measures of avoidance and emotional detachments, dissociative symptoms, such as inability to recall important aspects of the death, disbelief and denial over the death, "identification symptoms" whereby the widowed spouse reports the same pain and symptoms as that experienced by the deceased prior to his/her death. Traumatic grievers are also bothered by unbidden, intrusive thoughts of their deceased spouse that are frequent enough to impair daily functioning. Traumatic grief has been shown to be significantly associated with heightened arousal (e.g., increased blood pressure). Given that symptoms of grief have been found to persist for several years following the loss [9-11], traumatic grievers appear to meet the stipulation for "chronic" (i.e., duration lasting 3 months or more) rather than "acute" (i.e., duration lasting less than 3 months) PTSD. Traumatic grief has proven significantly associated with marked impairment in global, role, social, physical, and mental health functioning [2-4, 8]. Furthermore, traumatic grievers meet all the secondary criteria described as "Associated Features" (e.g., survivors guilt, hostility, feeling of constant threat, somatic complaints). Thus, despite the fact that bereavement is not typically considered by clinicians and standard diagnostic manuals to be an objectively traumatic events (i.e., akin to rape or concentration camp internment), bereaved individuals with traumatic grief do appear to meet the all the criteria necessary for a diagnosis of PTSD. We would like to demonstrate how an objectively less horrific event such as bereavement, nonetheless, results in posttraumatic symptomatology for certain vulnerable individuals.

In light of the findings demonstrating that traumatic grief is associated with a heightened risk of critical mental and physical health outcomes, it becomes important to try to understand the underlying mechanisms that may put individuals at risk of developing traumatic grief. Attachment theory as defined by Bowlby [12-14] helps to explain much of why bereavement may be traumatic for individuals who possess insecure attachments. Bowlby writes:

> Evidence at present available strongly suggests that adults whose mourning takes a pathological course are likely before their bereavement to have been prone to make affectional relationships of certain special, albeit contrasting, kinds. In one such group affectional relationships tend to be marketed by a high degree of anxious attachment, suffused with overt or covert ambivalence. In a second and related group there is a strong disposition to engage in compulsive caregiving. People in these groups are likely to be described as nervous, overdependent, clinging or temperamental, or else as neurotic. Some of them report having had a previous breakdown in which symptoms of anxiety or depression were prominent. In a third and contrasting group there are strenuous attempts to claim emotional self-sufficiency and independence of all affectional ties; through the very intensity with which the claims are made often reveals their precarious basis [14, p. 202].

From Bowlby's description, we might expect individuals with excessively dependent, compulsive caregiving, or defensively separated attachment styles to be more psychologically devastated by the loss of their spouse.

In this way, we concur with Bowlby's belief that the loss of a significant other might predispose insecurely attached individuals to any of several types of psychiatric disorders (e.g., anxiety, depression). However, we believe there is an additional, necessary component that needs to be taken into account in the development of traumatic grief. It does not appear to be simply the case that insecure or unstable attachments (including other personality traits described below) will result in traumatic grief, but rather that traumatic grievers are individuals with certain attachment/personality styles for whom marriage served a countervailing or compensatory function. Especially in situations in which the marriage was security-increasing, stabilizing and relatively exclusive, we would expect that individuals who are easily destabilized by separations from attachment figures (i.e., those with the attachment/personality styles identified here) would be psychologically *traumatized* by the loss. In some sense, for these individuals, the loss of the stabilizing relationship with the spouse puts them in the particularly precarious position of having lost the one person on whom they depended for support and whose presence and affection served to validate their sense of self.

As mentioned above, there are other vulnerability factors we believe would predispose to traumatic grief. After a review of our interviews with elderly spouses of the terminally ill and elderly widows and widowers, we have been struck by the frequency with which they display certain personality characteristics. These traits include a pattern of unstable self-image and affect often most pronounced in the period before marriage—the unstable self-image referring to the traumatic griever's uncertainty about his/her identity, goals and values; the unstable affect referring to his/her difficulty with modulating emotions, particularly, uncontrollable rage. Another prominent personality trait of traumatic grievers is their high susceptibility to separation-induced anxiety, with many becoming intensely and uncontrollably angry when they feel that a caregiver has neglected or abandoned them.

A model of our hypotheses might look like the one displayed in Figure 1, in which a history of childhood abuse or neglect, or extreme fluctuations in parenting could lead to insecure or unstable attachments and self-regulatory deficits such as an unstable identity, poor affect modulation, and an excessive fear of abandonment. Marriage to a supportive spouse relieves the sense of insecurity and instability by providing a desperately needed sense of reassurance. In this setting, loss of the stabilizing, relatively exclusive relationship (either through illness or death) is experienced as a psychological trauma which, in turn, results in traumatic grief. For these individuals, spousal loss resembles closely other types of trauma (e.g., rape, disaster exposure) and the experience of trauma produces the symptoms of pre- and post-loss traumatic grief and PTSD. Pre- and post-loss traumatic grief, and PTSD would then predict long-term mental and physical health impairments.

Our purpose here is to provide case histories that illustrate the clinical features of people with high levels of pre-loss grief (measured by the Inventory of Anticipatory Grief: IAG; [15] and post-loss traumatic grief (measured by the ICG). Although we present only three cases, we have found that many other traumatic grievers possess these same attachment/personality attributes. We wish to examine the fit between these cases and the model presented above. Three cases will be described in which insecure attachment styles (measured by the Relationship Styles Questionnaire: RSQ; [16], which is a self-report of extent to which the respondent feels they can identify with attachment styles such as compulsive caregiving, excessive dependency, antisocial features), personality characteristics (measured with the self-report items of the Structured Clinical Interview for the DSM-III (SCID-II); [17], such as obsessive-compulsive, borderline, histrionic, narcissistic features), and a prior history of childhood adversity or neglect are described among one anticipatory and two traumatic grievers (obtained from George Brown's Childhood Experience of Care and Abuse (CECA) interview schedule, including measures to determine whether the respondent had a history of sexual or physical abuse or parental neglect). Following the presentation of these three cases, the implications of attachment and personality characteristics for the treatment of traumatic grief will be discussed.

EXCESSIVE DEPENDENCY

Mr. R. is an eighty-one-year-old man who was referred approximately three months after his wife's death by his niece who had grown increasingly alarmed by his condition. At three months post-loss, Mr. R had an Inventory of Complicated Grief score that was quite elevated (ICG=40; ICG, and IAG, scores above 25 are in the "syndromal" range—mean = 18; st. dev. = 12 among persons

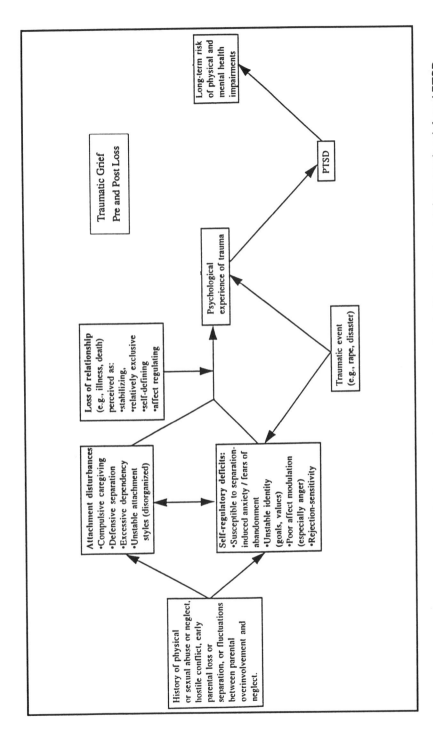

Figure 1. Hypothesized model of risk factors and outcomes associated with anticipatory grief, traumatic grief, and PTSD.

widowed an average of three years) with particular difficulties accepting his rage over the loss, preoccupation with thoughts of his wife to the point of impaired daily functioning, yearning and searching for his deceased wife, feeling disbelief and being stunned by her death, hopelessness, avoidance, and emptiness as a result of her death.

Mr. R's symptoms of traumatic grief may be better understood in the context of his underlying sense of inadequacy and the meaning of his relationship with his wife. During one session, he admitted to being very dependent on his wife throughout their lives to maintain good feelings about himself. Mr. R met his wife when they were in their early twenties. He described himself at that time as having no self-confidence and feeling very unattractive. He saw his wife as unusually attractive and popular with men. He pursued her and to his amazement, she agreed to marry him.

He was never able to explain what she saw in him, except that he was a nice guy. When pressed to explain why she agreed to marry him, he simply stated that she was a "gift from God," his "bashert," which in Yiddish means one's preordained soulmate, or each individual's one and only "true love." It seems that a common theme among bereaved people with traumatic grief reactions is the consideration of the death of their spouse as the loss of their one true love, the one with whom they were happy and without whom they feel, in some sense, even less than half of a whole. This is one of the important ways in which we believe the traumatic grief-prone relationship serves an identity-enhancing function.

To elaborate further on Mr. R's case, the sense that God had shown favor on him in his life seemed to be critical to his sense of well-being. In addition to the gift of his wonderful wife, he also felt that in combat during WWII, God had spared him from mortal wounds when others around him were dying. This self-focused, unilateral view of God may have been another manifestation of Mr. R's underdeveloped sense of himself and his own responsibility for his life. Thus, it seemed to him particularly cruel that God should with one stroke bless him with the gift of his wife and saving him from death, and with another stroke damn him by taking his wife away. He appeared to have conflicted feelings of rage and guilt at God for taking back his gift. Because of the unmodulated intensity, his therapist noted he had a great deal of difficulty expressing his anger. Difficulty modulating intense anger and other negative feelings is a characteristic of traumatic grievers.

Mr. R's dependency needs also emerged with his therapist. He would constantly seek reassurance from the therapist (e.g., "Are you getting tired of me yet? Isn't this frustrating for you, I don't seem to be making any progress with my loneliness"). When it was suggested to him that his therapy visits be reduced to every other week, he was very threatened by the thought of his therapy terminating, and suggested to the therapist that "even if you can't see it, the handwriting is on the wall. They are planning to get rid of me." Mr. R clearly had a strong fear of abandonment.

A final observation about the recollection of Mr. R's wife's death is of interest. When initially asked to recount the circumstances of his wife's death he indicated that his wife had died on the spot and that he was traumatized by the suddenness of her death. He offered no further details. However, months later, when the therapist asked him about the exact circumstances and actions he took when his wife had died, a totally different story emerged involving a wait for paramedics as she lay breathing, unconscious beside him. Mr. R's wife was transported to the nearest hospital and was then "life-flighted" to tertiary care facility; with Mr. R temporarily remaining unaware of the severity of her condition. Although Mr. R's wife was initially able to respond to simple commands in the ICU, her condition soon deteriorated and he elected to have her put on a respirator. Mr. R finally decided to withdraw her life support system and his wife died within fifteen minutes. It had taken an entire week from the time of her collapse until her death. The selective omissions and distortions of the trauma, denial, and an effort to avoid discussing the actual circumstances of her death, resemble the reaction often seen in patients with PTSD, and underscores the degree to which this type of loss is experienced as traumatic.

The case of Mr. R illustrates the possible association between personality characteristics such as excessive dependency, fears, and rage over abandonment by a "bashert" and traumatic grief. The distorted recollection and denial of the circumstances of his wife's death may be viewed as part of the dissociative phenomena that occur around the time of the trauma which Marmar et al. have found to predispose individuals to the development of PTSD [18]. These dissociative phenomena may prove to be useful markers for identifying who will be at greatest risk of developing traumatic grief.

COMPULSIVE CAREGIVING

Mrs. W is a seventy-five-year-old woman. She was initially interviewed six months before her husband passed away from esophageal cancer. Two months following the death of her spouse, she was reinterviewed over the telephone. Mrs. W was found to have an elevated Inventory of Anticipatory Grief score (IAG = 41; mean = 23; st. dev. = 15) at the first interview and a high Inventory of Complicated Grief score (ICG = 35) at the two month follow-up. It is noteworthy that she presented a similar symptom profile on both the IAG and ICG. Her major symptom complaints included preoccupation with thoughts of her husband to the point of distraction, avoidance of upsetting reminders related to her husband, being stunned or dazed over her husband's terminal illness and death, emptiness without him as he used to be, loneliness, and identification symptoms (sometimes referred to as "grief related facsimile illness"), auditory and visual hallucinations of her husband. Mrs. W's Hamilton Rating Scale for Depression (HRSD) score was a three at the first interview (in the "caregiver phase" of the study) and a five at the first follow-up two months after her husband's death. Each of these ratings are well below the HRSD scores associated with clinical depression, even at the subsyndromal level.

Mrs. W exhibited personality traits that were indicative of compulsive caregiving and defensive separation. These characteristics appeared to be related to experiences in her childhood and early adulthood. Mrs. W and her two sisters were responsible for caring for their mother through most of their childhood. Due to serious health difficulties, their mother was unable to run the household and the bulk of the responsibilities for maintaining the household and supporting the mother fell on Mrs. W, who was the oldest daughter. Moreover, her father, a strict Catholic, insisted that his daughters take care of him and their six brothers. Thus, role reversal with her mother was a prominent feature of Mrs. W's childhood and often resulted in her own needs being neglected.

Although she stated that she enjoyed caring for others, she also described elements of defensive separation (cf. Bowlby [14]) such as not wanting to take orders, rooted in her wish to rebel against her strict, domineering father. Similarly, she endorsed items suggesting that she did not like to commit to things because she would not feel that she could then change her mind. Mrs. W also reported that she becomes very angry when she feels that she is being rejected or neglected in some way—a characteristic often seen in defensively separated individuals. Mrs. W left home at the age of eighteen to join the Navy Nursing Corps in order to escape from the strict household run by her father. She was stationed in the South Pacific from 1942 until 1946. While in the South Pacific, Mrs. W witnessed the casualties of war; as a nurse she treated seamen and marines who had been wounded in the fierce fighting throughout that area.

In 1955 when she was about to retire from the Navy, Mrs. W met her husband and they were married within six months. They remained married for forty years up until the time of his death. Mrs. W described her marriage in exclusively positive terms. She described how he had been her best friend and confidante throughout their entire marriage, with no separations, ongoing tensions or conflicts. In 1992 when Mrs. W had a stroke, her husband was very supportive, and assisted with her rehabilitation. She stated that "if it was not for him I would not have survived the stroke." After his illness began, Mrs. W returned to her role as caregiver; this time to her husband. She commented that she enjoyed caregiving in her childhood and that was the reason she chose nursing as a career. Mrs. W clearly seemed to thrive in her role as a caregiver.

At the time of the second interview, Mrs. W stated that she was withdrawing from the study because she did not want to be reminded of her husband. Her therapist believed that her withdrawal was an attempt to avoid confronting emotions provoked by the death of her husband.

The case of Mrs. W illustrates again the central role of a stabilizing relationship. It further suggests that an early childhood experience of role reversal and, consequent neglect, together with open hostility from an excessively demanding, uncaring father might be related to rejection-sensitivity and two, seemingly contradictory, attachment styles: compulsive caregiving and defensive separation. Oscillation between these attachment styles may have been an outgrowth of fluctuations between "overcontrol" and "neglect" she had experienced in her youth. Of interest Mrs. W, like Mr. R, was exposed to the trauma of war casualties. Heidi Resnick (personal communication) has found prior exposure to trauma to be a risk factor for PTSD. This may prove similarly to be an underlying vulnerability factor for traumatic grief.

EXCESSIVE FEAR OF ABANDONMENT

Mrs. C is a sixty-three-year-old woman married to the same man for forty-four years. Mrs. C was interviewed nine months following her husband's diagnosis of a malignant brain tumor which metastasized to multiple regions of his body. For the three months prior to the interview, she reported that her husband's condition appeared to be steadily improving, even though his condition was still considered to be terminal.

Mrs. C described her relationship with her husband as being quite good. They rarely, if ever, argued and there was no reported history of any abuse or infidelity from either partner. Before her husband's illness, Mrs. C stated that she and her husband would spend a great deal of time doing things as a couple (e.g., traveling, working around the house). Prior to her husband's retirement, she was the office administrator for her husband's business. She described their preference to spend a lot of time together as being consistent throughout their entire marriage.

Mrs. C presented in the interview with no major or subsyndromal depression (HRSD = 3), or dysthymia and did not meet DSM-IV criteria for any anxiety or mood disorders. However, she did display one of the most intense anticipatory grief reaction scores (IAG = 55) we have encountered. Mrs. C exhibited each of the symptoms of anticipatory grief to some degree. Most notably, she displayed extreme bitterness and anger over her husband's illness, having felt that it was unfair that he should have become so ill. She was also constantly preoccupied with thoughts of her husband, had visual and auditory hallucinations of her husband, and did report experiencing some of the same symptoms as those that troubled her husband. In addition to these symptoms, she also expressed a lack of trust in people and an inability to care for people with whom she had formerly felt very close.

Aside from the anticipatory grief reaction, Mrs. C endorsed self-regulatory deficits displayed in our model. She described herself as impulsive, confused over long-term goals, becoming extremely upset when a person she cared about was going to leave, and becoming enraged when she felt someone had slighted her.

Mrs. C. reported parental verbal abuse, strappings, hostility, and neglect. The family in which she grew up was extremely poor, often not having enough money for food or clothes. Her father was out of work for extended periods of time due to poor health. Her mother was also quite ill and unable to supplement the family income. From the time she was eight until the time of her marriage, she was responsible for running the household (e.g., cleaning, cooking, washing, etc.). These chores severely constrained her social life by not allowing her time to have or maintain friendships.

Mrs. C had a difficult relationship with her father. She remembers him as being very critical of her entire family. He seemed disinterested in her personal aims or wishes, never caring about how she was performing in school or any difficulties she was having. She stated that her father cared only about things that affected him directly. Mrs. C's father was a harsh disciplinarian, becoming verbally abusive if she did not perform to his satisfaction (i.e., he would tell her how stupid she was or make some derogatory comments about her appearance). Often she would be typically punished by being hit repeatedly with a leather belt over her entire body.

Mrs. C remembered a more positive relationship with her mother who was her primary confidante. However, she stated that her mother would cry to her every day about her father and his poor treatment of the family. At times, she reported being made to feel guilty that she was not taking enough responsibility for the family, even though she was running the household.

The case of Mrs. C illustrates a third time the central role of a very positive, supportive, relatively exclusive long-term relationship. We also learn from Mrs. C how an experience with physical and verbal abuse and neglect as a child might be associated with the later emergence of personality traits of impulsivity, confusion over their long-term goals and identity, susceptibility to separation-induced anxiety, and anger at the perception of rejection by a significant other. Given her intense fear of abandonment, it was not surprising that she experienced severe anticipatory grief in reaction to both the loss of her husband as she had known him and his impending death.

DISCUSSION

We present here three cases of anticipatory and traumatic grief in which a central feature was loss of an unusually strong and gratifying long-term friendship. Freud had postulated that ambivalent or conflictual marriages would result in depression or anxiety following the death of one's spouse [19]. However, preliminary evidence suggests that while conflictual marriages may indeed put widows and widowers at heightened risk of bereavement-related depression or anxiety, they do *not* predispose to traumatic grief. Rather, it has been our repeated observation that the reverse is true; that is, that widowed persons having had unusually good, long-term, and relatively exclusive marriages are those who appear to experience traumatic grief.

Unlike Freud, Bowlby postulated that the nature of the underlying attachment would determine the response to grief, regardless of the degree of conflict.

However, Bowlby did not distinguish different types of pathological mourning or the way the loss of an attachment that served to compensate for early attachment disturbances might result in psychological trauma. We have identified a specific type of pathological grief reaction characterized by symptoms which resemble PTSD. This traumatic grief reaction appears to occur most often in a clinical situation with the following characteristics: 1) evidence of a disturbance in attachment; 2) personality traits indicative of self-regulatory deficits; and 3) loss of an unusually stabilizing, identity-enhancing, relatively exclusive relationship. Individuals who fit this profile appear to be particularly vulnerable to, or "traumatized" by, the loss of the attachment upon whom they depended, in some sense, for their very survival.

Our conclusion from our initial observations is that the nature of an individual's attachment relationships critically influences the propensity to develop traumatic grief. As such, attachment concepts appear to be useful in understanding the genesis of traumatic grief. Several other studies support the idea that there may be a connection between the strength of an attachment and intensity of the grief or posttraumatic stress reaction. Brent et al. found in a study of adolescent witnesses to suicide that both PTSD symptoms and symptoms of grief were correlated with the closeness to an interdependency with the suicide victims [20]. In a recent Dutch study, it was found that a relatively long length of pregnancy (gestational age) and the absence of children at the time of the miscarriage were among the most important risk factors for stronger grief responses in women following pregnancy loss [21]. This would suggest that the grief reaction was related to the attachment to the unborn fetus; that is, the older the gestational age at the time of miscarriage, the stronger the attachment to the fetus, and the greater the sense of loss, especially if the woman had no other living children at home to buffer the sense of loss. Intensity of attachment to the deceased, especially when this attachment serves to compensate for an underlying weakness in self-regulatory mechanisms, appears to be related to the degree to which the bereaved will suffer from traumatic grief.

Attachment theory allows for connections to be made between early interpersonal experiences and the formation of specific "internal working models" [12] that characterize life-long attachment styles and personality types. A history of childhood adversity or neglect has been shown to result in the development of attachment disturbances, such as excessive dependency, defensive separation, and compulsive caregiving [12]. Early adversity and/or attachment disturbances may also interfere with development of healthy self-regulatory mechanisms. Other researchers describe how physical abuse, early separation or loss, and parental overcontrol may predispose people to personality disorders [22, 23]. The cases described above are consistent with the idea that individuals with insecure attachments and with self-regulatory deficits had life experiences which shaped their cognitive sets. We hypothesize that a stabilizing adult relationship can serve an identity-enhancing function, compensating for the destabilizing effects of underlying, maladaptive cognitive sets. Loss of this security-increasing, stabilizing relationship is then experienced as a psychological trauma.

Internal working models are increasingly of interest to Cognitive-Behavioral Therapies [CBT; 24-26]. However, correction of distortions associated with the insecure attachment styles have not been a focus of much CBT work to date. We believe that attention to cognitive aspects of attachment and self-regulation which seem to predispose to traumatic grief may prove to be a worthwhile focus of treatment. For example, the belief of an excessively dependent individual, and/or those with extreme fears of abandonment, that they will not be able to survive without the presence of their deceased loved one may be related to threatened emergence of uncontrollable affect, or other self-regulatory deficits. The therapeutic work would center on identifying and strengthening these underdeveloped regulatory processes. Compulsive caregivers may define their identity and/or life goals only in relation to the needs of their spouse. The therapist might work with these patients to help them to develop independent goals and a stable sense of their own identity. For traumatic grievers with defensively separated attachment styles, fears may center on a feeling of engulfment or hypersensitivity to rejection. Again, the therapist must work on enhancing self-regulatory functioning such that there is a greater sense of internal consistency in the face of demands and changes in external relationships. As these various self-regulatory mechanisms are put into place, traumatic grief sufferers may be able to put the deceased and their relationship to him/her in a more realistic light. It is our hope that attention to attachment disturbances, self-regulatory deficits, and the function of stabilizing relationships promise greater insight into the etiology and, ultimately, treatment of traumatic grief.

REFERENCES

1. American Psychiatric Association, *DSM-IV*, American Psychiatric Association, Washington, D.C., 1994.
2. H. G. Prigerson, E. Frank, S. V. Kasl, et al., Complicated Grief and Bereavement-Related Depression as Distinct Disorders: Preliminary Empirical Validation in Elderly Bereaved Spouses, *American Journal of Psychiatry 152*:1, pp. 22-30, 1995.
3. H. G. Prigerson, M. K. Shear, J. T. Newsom et al., Anxiety among Widowed Elders: Is it Distinct from Depression and Grief? *Anxiety, 2,* pp. 1-12, 1996.
4. H. G. Prigerson, S. V. Kasl, C. F. Reynolds, III, A. J. Bierhals, E. Frank, and S. Jacobs, Traumatic Grief as a Risk Factor for Mental and Physical Morbidity, *American Journal of Psychiatry*, 1997.
5. L. C. Beery, H. G. Prigerson, A. J. Bierhals, L. Santucci, J. T. Newsom, Traumatic Grief, Depression, and Caregiving in Elderly Spouses of the Terminally Ill, *Omega: Journal of Death and Dying*, 1997.
6. T. R. Fashingbauer, S. Zisook, R. De Vaul et al., The Texas Revised Inventory of Grief, in *Biopsychosocial Aspects of Bereavement*, S. Zisook (ed.), American Psychiatric Press, Inc. Washington, D.C., 1987.

7. S. Jacobs, F. Hansen, S. V. Kasl et al., The Measurement of Grief: Bereaved versus Non-Bereaved, *The Hospice Journal, 2*, pp. 21-36, 1987.
8. H. G. Prigerson, P. K. Maciejewski, C. F. Reynolds III et al., The Inventory of Complicated Grief: A Scale to Measure Certain Maladaptive Symptoms of Loss, *Psychiatry Research, 59*, pp. 65-79, 1995.
9. A. J. Bierhals, H. G. Prigerson, A. Fasiczka, E. Frank, M. D. Miller, and C. F. Reynolds III, Gender Differences in Complicated Grief among the Elderly, *Omega: Journal of Death and Dying, 32*:4, pp. 303-317, 1996.
10. S. C. Jacobs, S. V. Kasl, A. M. Ostfeld et al., The Measurement of Grief: Bereaved versus Non-Bereaved, *The Hospice Journal, 2*, pp. 21-36, 1986.
11. R. E. Pasternak, C. F. Reynolds III, M. Schlerntizauer et al., Acute Open-Trial Nortriptyline Therapy of Bereavement-Related Depression in Late Life, *Journal of Clinical Psychiatry, 52*, pp. 307-310, 1991.
12. J. Bowlby, *Attachment and Loss, Vol. 1. Attachment*, Basic Books, New York, 1969.
13. J. Bowlby, *Attachment and Loss, Vol. 2: Separation, Anxiety and Anger*, Hogarth Press, London, 1973.
14. J. Bowlby, *Attachment and Loss, Vol. 3: Loss*, Basic Books Inc., New York, 1980.
15. H. G. Prigerson, M. Miller, E. Frank, R. Schulz, E. Heskey, and C. F. Reynolds III, *Inventory of Anticipatory Grief*, unpublished, 1995.
16. P. Pilkonis, H. G. Prigerson, and E. Frank, Relationship Styles Questionnaire, unpublished, 1994.
17. R. L. Spitzer, J. B. Williams, M. Gibbon et al., *Structured Clinical Interview for the DSM-III-R: Non-Patient Edition*, Biometrics Research Department, New York State Psychiatric Institute, New York, 1989.
18. C. R. Marmar, D. S. Weiss, W. E. Schlenger et al., Peritraumatic Dissociation and Posttraumatic Stress in Male Vietnam Theater Veterans, *American Journal of Psychiatry, 151*:6, pp. 902-907, 1994.
19. S. Freud, Mourning and Melancholia, *International Zeitschrift fur arzliche Psychoanalyse, 4*, pp. 288-301, 1917.
20. D. A. Brent, J. Perper, G. Moritz et al., Adolescent Witnesses to a Peer Suicide, *Journal of the American Academy of Child and Adolescent Psychiatry, 32*:6, pp. 1184-1188, 1993.
21. H. Janssen, M. Curisnier, K. de Graauw, and K. Hoogduin, A Prospective Study of Risk Factors Predicting Grief Intensity following Pregnancy Loss, *Archives of General Psychiatry, 54*, pp. 56-61, January 1997.
22. J. Paris, H. Zweig-Frank, and J. Guzder, Risk Factors for Borderline Personality in Male Outpatients, *Journal of Nervous & Mental Disease, 182*:7, pp. 375-380, 1994.
23. M. Patrick, P. R. Hobson, D. Castle et al., Personality Disorder and the Mental Representation of Early Social Experience, *Development & Psychopathology, 6*:2, pp. 374-388, 1994.
24. A. T. Beck, A. Rush, B. Shaw et al., *Cognitive-Therapy of Depression*, Guilford Press, New York, 1979.
25. C. J. Robins and A. M. Hayes, An Appraisal of Cognitive Therapy, *Journal of Consulting and Clinical Psychology, 61*, pp. 205-214, 1993.

26. J. Teasdale, Emotion and Two Kinds of Meaning: Therapy and Applied Cognitive Science, *Behavior Research and Therapy, 31*, pp. 339-354, 1993.

SIBLING BEREAVEMENT IN LATE LIFE*

JUDITH C. HAYS, R.N., PH.D.
DEBORAH T. GOLD, PH.D.
CARL F. PIEPER, DR.PH.
Duke Medical Center, Durham, North Carolina

ABSTRACT

Elders are more likely to confront the death of a sibling than any other kinship bereavement. Yet we know almost nothing about the impact of sibling deaths on older adults. We used attachment theory to generate hypotheses about the impact of this life event on physical health, mood, social support, and economic outcomes in late life. At the Duke University site of a large multi-center epidemiologic study (EPESE), 3173 elderly community-dwellers provided data on bereavements experienced in the past year as well as on demographic, health-related, and socioeconomic characteristics. Bereaved siblings were more functionally and cognitively impaired than bereaved friends and rated their overall health as worse than bereaved spouses or bereaved friends who were similarly impaired. Brothers and sisters bereaved of a brother reported excess financial hardship and mood impairment, respectively. Terminal care programs should screen for excess risk among surviving siblings and plan for assisting these survivors in adaptation to this loss.

---

*The research upon which this publication was based was performed pursuant to the National Institutes of Health's National Institute on Aging Contract Numbers N01-AG-1-2102 in support of the Established Populations for Epidemiological Studies of the Elderly (Duke) and P60-AG-1-1268 in support of the Claude D. Pepper Older Americans Independence Center, and National Institute on Mental Health Grant Number MH-44716 in support of the Mental Health Clinical Research Center for the Study of Depression in Late Life. The content of this publication does not necessarily reflect the views or policies of the U.S. Department of Health and Human Services.

© 1997, Baywood Publishing Co., Inc.

> One husband gone I might have found another,
> or a child from a new man in first child's place,
> but with my parents hid away in death,
> no brother, ever, could spring up for me.
>
> *Antigone*

Sophocles' Antigone is younger by far than the bereaved siblings whom we will consider in this article. But her great grief at the simultaneous loss of her two brothers and her willingness to sacrifice her own life that theirs might be suitably honored points us toward the study of a particular human attachment which has received strikingly little attention from scholars of bereavement.

There is a small but growing literature on sibling relationships in later life, generated, perhaps, by the fact that the Baby Boom will be the first cohort that has more siblings than children [1]. As the members of this large cohort age, they may need to look for social or material support from horizontal relations (i.e., siblings) as well as from vertical ones (i.e., children) [2]. In general, studies of siblings in late life have relied on small samples, convenient for the qualitative examination of the nature and meaning of the sibling relationships of the elderly. Although one investigator used a population-based sample to examine sibling relations [3], that sample was Canadian and may not be generalizable to the United States experience because of varying patterns of migration, health service availability, and family structure [4].

Siblings serve as a major resource for life review among older adults [3]. This shared developmental task would naturally be interrupted with the death of one of the siblings. In fact, elders are more likely to confront the death of a sibling than of any other kin. Quantifying the prevalence of sibling bereavement is complicated by the fact that census data does not count sibling deaths, and few studies of late-life siblings focus on the issue of death. Only one previous study of older adults' sibling relations focused on research questions about sibling deaths, and the investigators relied on semi-structured interviews with small numbers of older adults [5]. Sample size obviously precluded quantitative analysis of these data. Two other studies, concentrating on the special sibling relationship of twins, found that the death of one adult twin was profoundly disruptive to the emotional and functional state of the surviving twin [6, 7]. Only one study of adaptation to bereavement focused on the death of an adult sibling. Cleiren reported from the Leiden (Holland) Bereavement Study that adaptation to the death of an adult sibling was more difficult than adaptation to the death of a spouse, with particular risk to bereaved sisters [8]. Ross and Milgram [9] and Gold [10-12] note that over time the intensity of most sibling relationships follows a U-shaped curve, with the highest interest and involvement in childhood and late life. Thus, the strengthening of bonds between siblings in late life could make the loss of a sibling far more consequential than it would have been earlier in life.

Bowlby's theory of attachment suggests why sibling deaths may be stressful [13]. Siblings—like mother and child—form emotional bonds early in life based on mutual affection and reciprocal support. Gold and colleagues demonstrated that the attachment bonds between elderly siblings could be either positive or negative; regardless of the emotional valence, they are exceptionally strong and do not require constant contact or physical proximity for their maintenance as friendships might [14]. In Gold's typology of sibling relationships, only 10 percent of the respondents reported apathetic or disinterested attitudes toward siblings. All other types revealed long-term attachments, with 80 percent of those being positive attachments. This pattern held true among African-American siblings as well as Caucasian siblings [15]. On the other hand, Weiss [16] cautions that sibling bonds may be more "relationships of community" than "relationships of attachment." In contrast to Antigone, he proposes that "the death of a spouse or a child tends to be followed by years of grief; the death of a friend . . . or an adult sibling living in a different household tends to be followed by distress and sadness but not by severe persisting grief" [16, p. 271]. While there is debate about the emotional impact of sibling death, the literature is silent concerning the financial or instrumental hardship which might result from loss of a sibling.

Our empirical study of sibling bereavement—like the extensive study of spousal bereavement—will set these theoretical questions in the context of a model of stress and coping (Figure 1) [17], and use epidemiologic data to test hypotheses predicated on their tenets. The Established Populations for the Epidemiologic Study of the Elderly (EPESE) at Duke University provides not only a large population-based, biracial sample of rural and urban elders but also includes respondent data on the appraisal of recent negative life events as well as a wide range of psychosocial and economic outcome variables.

We compared the appraisal and outcomes of bereavement among three groups: bereaved siblings, bereaved spouses, and bereaved friends. Based on the literature described above, we hypothesized that each type of bereavement would be appraised as primarily negative although for different reasons. Sibling bereavement may pose a threat to both one's mood state, i.e., by disrupting the longest-lived of late-life relationships and the processes of life review, and also to the overall evaluation of one's health and well-being. Spousal bereavement may alter mood and physical health status by disrupting the most highly entrained relationship of late life, i.e., by destabilizing the life-supporting social and biological rhythms which are based on multiple cues sent and received by partners in a shared domicile over many years [18]. Spousal bereavement is also more likely than sibling bereavement to be associated with financial hardship, particularly among elderly women. Friendship bereavement in late life disrupts perhaps the most intentional of the three types of relationships, in that the maintenance of a friendship is not dictated by a blood relationship nor by a marriage contract made in earlier adulthood, and so may also be associated with mood disruption.

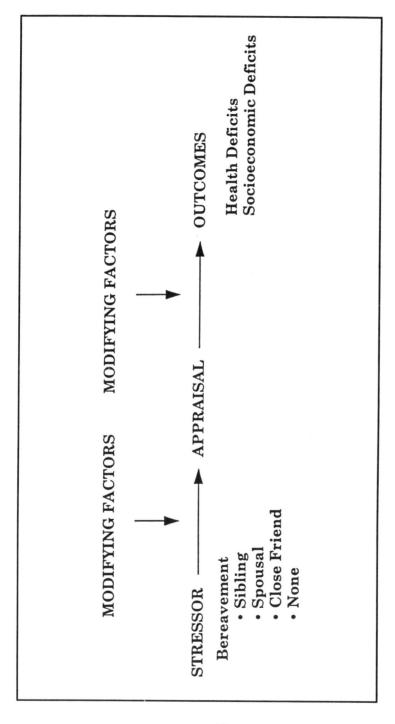

Figure 1. Hypothesized relationships among a bereavement event, its appraisal, and various health-related and socioeconomic outcomes, as potentially modified by selected characteristics and testable in future research.

Our research questions included:

- What is the frequency of sibling bereavement in a community sample of elderly adults?
- Compared to other kinds of bereavement, in which age, gender, and racial groups is sibling bereavement most common?

Our research hypotheses included:

- There will be no difference in the appraisal of the overall impact of bereavement across bereavement groups.
- Physical health deficits will characterize sibling and spousal bereaved more than friend bereaved.
- Mood differences and satisfaction with social support will not distinguish the three bereavement groups.
- Socioeconomic problems will characterize spousal bereaved more than sibling or friend bereaved, particularly among women.

METHODS

Sample

The Established Populations for Epidemiologic Studies of the Elderly (EPESE) project at Duke University Medical Center provided the data used for this study. The data were collected as part of a multi-center collaborative epidemiologic investigation of health status and the physical, social, and cognitive functioning of persons sixty-five years of age and older living in four communities: East Boston, Massachusetts; Iowa and Washington Counties, Iowa; New Haven, Connecticut; and five counties in the north central North Carolina Piedmont area [19].

Data from the North Carolina sample only were used for these analyses. The sample includes 4,162 non-institutionalized elderly respondents with approximately equal numbers of rural and urban dwellers and an oversample of Black elders. Sample members provided baseline data in 1986 and were re-interviewed in each of the following three years. At the fourth contact (1989), 72 percent of the sample ($n = 3173$) provided data on four types of bereavements experienced in the past year. The major reasons for non-response were mortality and missing data related to the interview having been administered to a proxy respondent.

Measures

Bereavement experience was assessed with four items which asked about deaths in the past year, including how many months prior to the interview each death had occurred. The respondent was asked directly about loss of a friend, spouse, child, or other relative. Loss of a sibling came from a follow-up question which allowed the respondent to answer one from eight possible relatives other than a spouse or child. For each reported death, the sample member evaluated the effect of that death on himself or herself as "negative," "neutral/mixed," or "positive."

Demographic variables included age, race, and gender. Health-related risk factors included seven scales. Deficits in physical activities of daily living or physical functioning were measured by the Katz [20] and Nagi [21] scales, respectively. The Katz scale (range = 0-5; sample mean [$s.d.$] = 0.18[0.70]) reflects need for assistance in bathing, dressing, eating, bed-to-chair transfers, and toileting. The Nagi scale (range = 0-4; sample mean [$s.d.$] = 0.98[1.32]) reflects difficulty moving a large object, stooping, carrying ten pounds, or reaching above the shoulder. Cognitive function was measured by the number of errors recorded on the Short Portable Mental Status Questionnaire (SPMSQ) [22] and taps domains such as memory, orientation, and concentration (range = 0-10; sample means [$s.d.$] = 1.72[1.77]). Mood impairment was measured by the twenty-item Center for Epidemiologic Studies—Depression scale (CES-D) [23] and included items reflecting positive and negative affect, somatic complaints, and interpersonal problems (range = 0-20; sample means [$s.d.$] = 3.12[3.33]). A global self-rating of health scale (excellent, good, fair, or poor) [24] and number of hospitalizations in the past year were also examined (range = 0-8; sample means [$s.d.$] = 0.21[0.60]). A life satisfaction scale [25] was also included, using fourteen yes-or-no items, such as "These are the best years of my life." The range of the life satisfaction scale was 0-26, and the sample mean [$s.d.$] was 18.15 [4.92].

Social and economic risk factors were measured with four scales. Internal locus of control [26] was assessed with an eight-item scale (range = 0-8; sample mean [$s.d.$] = 4.03[1.69]), including items such as, "What happens to me in the future mostly depends on me." Perceived adequacy of social support was measured as the sum of two three-level items (range 2-6; sample mean [$s.d.$] = 5.50[0.91]) which tap the degree to which a respondent perceives that she or he has a confidant or someone to provide support in difficult times [27]. Two items indexed the adequacy of financial resources for meeting "needs" (poorly, fairly well, very well) and "emergencies" (yes, no), respectively.

Analysis

The analyses used a retrospective cohort design with four exposure groups. The sibling bereavement exposure group consisted of all persons who reported the death of only a brother or a sister in the previous year. The spousal bereavement exposure group included those who reported the death of a spouse but not a sibling, child, or friend. The friend bereavement exposure group included those who reported the death of a friend but not a spouse, sibling, or child. A non-bereaved exposure group was constructed of persons who reported no bereavement of any kind in the previous year. Removed from group analyses were 1) respondents bereaved of a child ($n = 29$), 2) respondents bereaved of only a son-in-law, daughter-in-law, grandchild, parent, niece, nephew, cousin, or other close relative besides a spouse or sibling ($n = 387$), and 3) all respondents who reported the recent death of two or more of the following: sibling, spouse, child, or friend ($n = 131$).

Exposure groups were constructed separately for men and women based on the widely documented gender differences in bereavement-related outcomes [16]. Demographic data are provided for the total sample ($n = 3173$). Exposure groups were compared on age, race, the number of months since the index bereavement, and the appraisal of the loss by the survivor.

Exposure groups were also compared on all outcomes, using analyses of covariance (ANCOVA). Outcomes measured at follow-up in 1989 were adjusted for baseline (1986) level of that variable and for age. In addition, cognitive impairment was adjusted for education and race, and self-rated health was adjusted for concurrent activities of daily living, cognitive impairment, and depression. Omnibus F-tests for between-group differences were conducted, using a cut-off for significance of $p \leq 0.05$. When the model F demonstrated significance, we compared group means pairwise (i.e., sibling bereaved against each other group), in order to control against Type I. The cut-off level for significance was lowered to $p \leq 0.0167$ (0.05 ÷ 3 comparisons), the traditional cut-off level divided by the number of comparisons. Chi-square tests were used to test for independence of categorical-level outcome variables across groups.

RESULTS

Demographic characteristics and bereavement experience of the sample is shown in Table 1. The extent of sibling bereavement over one year in this population was close to 10 percent. Approximately 6 to 7 percent of elderly men and women in the sample reported the death of a sibling only during the year before the interview. An additional 3 percent of women ($n = 66$) and 3 percent of men ($n = 33$) reported multiple deaths including that of a sibling. At the same interview, 1 to 2 percent of the sample reported only the death of a spouse. An additional 0.6 percent of women ($n = 12$) and 0.9 percent of men ($n = 9$) reported multiple deaths including that of a spouse. Between 25 to 31 percent of subjects reported the death of a friend. Nearly half of the sample did not report any bereavement experience in the year prior to the interview.

Age, race, and appraisal differences across the exposure groups are shown in Table 2. Elders who experienced a sibling bereavement were approximately the same age as elders who experienced death of a spouse or friend, although there was a trend for recent widowers to be slightly older than the other exposure groups. All bereavement losses were similarly distributed among Black and White sample members.

Table 1. Characteristics of the Sample:
Bereavement Experience, Age, and Race, Separately for Men and Women

Characteristics	Women (n = 2132)		Men (n = 1041)	
	n	(%)[a]	n	(%)[a]
Bereavement Experience				
Sister only[b]	59	(2.7)	27	(3.1)
Brother only[b]	66	(2.9)	47	(4.3)
Spouse only[c]	17	(1.1)	11	(1.6)
Close friend only[d]	405	(19.5)	250	(24.2)
Child only	25	(1.2)	4	(0.3)
Son/Daughter-in-law only	11	(0.5)	0	—
Grandchild only	11	(0.3)	3	(0.3)
Parent only	11	(0.8)	2	(0.2)
Niece/Nephew only	63	(2.2)	13	(1.3)
Cousin only	79	(3.1)	23	(1.7)
Other relative only	117	(6.5)	54	(5.5)
Spouse + 1 non-sib relative[c]	4	(0.3)	1	(0.1)
Friend + 1 non-sib relative[d]	138	(5.7)	69	(6.5)
Multiple inc. 2 + FrSpSib	87	(4.0)	44	(4.2)
No bereavement	1039	(49.4)	493	(46.8)
Age Group				
67-74	896	(45.5)	615	(54.5)
75-84	939	(42.8)	352	(38.7)
85+	297	(11.8)	74	(6.8)
Race				
White	951	(64.2)	476	(64.8)
Black	1181	(35.8)	565	(35.2)

[a]Frequencies are unweighted; percentages are weighted.
[b]Sibling (case) group includes sample members bereaved of brother only or sister only.
[c]Spouse (control) group includes sample members bereaved of spouse only and those bereaved of a spouse and one non-sibling, non-child relative.
[d]Friend (control) group includes sample members bereaved of close friend only and those bereaved of a close friend and a non-spouse, non-sibling, non-child relative.

Bereaved siblings were more likely than bereaved spouses or friends to report that the death had a positive effect on them, as compared to a neutral or negative effect. At the same time, widows and widowers were more likely to evaluate the effect of their bereavements as negative, and bereaved friends experienced more neutral/mixed effects than would be expected by chance. Because the effect of a bereavement might be attributable to its temporal proximity, we examined the average number of months elapsed since the deaths of siblings, spouses, and

Table 2. Differences in Bereavement Experience by Age, Racial Group, and Effect on Survivors, Separately for Men and Women

Bereavement Experience	n	Age Mean	(s.e.)	Race Black ($n = 803$) %	Race White ($n = 925$) %	Effect Neg ($n = 377$) %	Effect Neu/Mix ($n = 224$) %	Effect Pos ($n = 36$) %
\multicolumn{9}{c}{Women ($n = 1728$)}
Sibling	118	72.95	(0.58)	7.9	6.3	17.0	10.5	27.8
Spouse	29	72.88	(1.17)	1.6	1.6	5.5	3.4	0.0
Friend	534	72.95	(0.28)	32.5	30.1	77.5	86.1	72.2
None	1147	73.33	(0.20)	58.0	61.2	—	—	—
F(p)		0.50 (0.69)		—		—		
LRX² (p)		—		3.2 (.36)		12.6 (.01)		

Bereavement Experience	n	Age Mean	(s.e.)	Race Black ($n = 414$) %	Race White ($n = 484$) %	Effect Neg ($n = 174$) %	Effect Neu/Mix ($n = 180$) %	Effect Pos ($n = 28$) %
\multicolumn{9}{c}{Men ($n = 898$)}
Sibling	76	71.80	(0.66)	7.9	8.8	20.0	11.4	34.2
Spouse	17	75.11	(1.39)	1.0	2.6	8.0	0.5	6.5
Friend	319	71.77	(0.32)	36.5	34.9	72.0	88.1	59.3
None	486	72.38	(0.26)	54.8	53.7	—	—	—
F(p)		2.33 (0.07)		—		—		
LRX² (p)		—		4.3 (.23)		26.4 (.00)		

friends. In data not shown, bereaved friends reported the fewest number of months since the index death which would be expected since adults have many more friends than spouses or siblings; siblings and spouses had similar times since their index bereavements. We also examined the average number of months elapsed since bereavement according to the effect of the death and found that time elapsed since the index bereavement was not significantly related to appraisal across the three survivor groups (data not shown).

Elderly bereaved sisters reported more ADL deficits and made significantly more errors on the SPMSQ than elderly women who were bereaved of friends (Table 3). Bereaved sisters also evaluated their overall health as significantly worse than widows. There were no appreciable differences in other physical health or mood problems or in the social or economic resources available to these groups of women.

Table 3. Differences in Health, Social, and Economic Resource Deficits across Bereavement Groups: Women

	Women: Bereavement Experience[a]								Significant Differences
	Sibling		Spouse		Friend		None		
Characteristic	X̄(se)	%	X̄(se)	%	X̄(se)	%	X̄(se)	%	Sibs vs. Others[b]
Health Deficits									
ADL deficits	0.72 (.09)		0.60 (.18)		0.40 (.04)		0.54 (.03)		Sibs > Fr
Nagi deficits	1.30 (.12)		1.64 (.21)		1.40 (.05)		1.40 (.04)		NS
Hospitalizations (past yr.)	0.34 (.06)		0.17 (.13)		0.29 (.03)		0.23 (.02)		NS
CESD score	3.18 (.31)		3.16 (.57)		3.17 (.14)		2.67 (.10)		NS
SPMSQ errors[c]	2.38 (.16)		1.78 (.32)		1.69 (.08)		2.11 (.06)		Sibs > Fr
Poor SRH[d]	2.76 (.08)		2.28 (.17)		2.73 (.04)		2.70 (.03)		Sibs > Sp
Life satisfaction	18.23 (.47)		17.64 (.91)		17.87 (.21)		18.06 (.16)		NS
Social and Economic Deficits									
Perceived support	5.63 (.08)		5.81 (.16)		5.51 (.04)		5.53 (.03)		NS
Locus of control (internal)	4.06 (.16)		4.05 (.50)		3.75 (.07)		4.11 (.06)		NS
Enough $ for needs									NS
Poorly		15.0		4.6		12.2		14.0	
Fairly well		48.1		49.9		49.3		45.3	
Very well		36.9		45.5		38.5		40.7	
Enough $ for emergencies									NS
No		28.0		12.7		29.7		29.8	
Yes		72.0		87.3		70.3		70.2	

[a] All means are from 1989 adjusted for baseline scores from 1986 and age, except Locus of control which was not included in the baseline interview.
[b] Significant differences include pairwise differences in mean scores or proportions between sibling bereaved and any of the three comparison groups where $p \leq 0.0167$ (= 0.05 ÷ 3 comparisons).

Elderly bereaved brothers also reported more ADL deficits and more errors on the SPMSQ than elderly men bereaved of friends (Table 4). Moreover, their self-rated health was the worst of any other exposure group—significantly worse than widowers or men bereaved of friends. However, widowers and bereaved friends reported more mood impairment than bereaved brothers, and widowers were significantly less satisfied with their social support than bereaved brothers. The groups were similar with respect to economic resources.

In general, differences in the outcomes of the loss of a brother compared to the loss of a sister were trivial, with two exceptions (data not shown). There was a trend among bereaved sisters who lost a brother to experience more depressive symptomatology than did sisters who lost a sister. A similar trend suggested that the loss of a brother depleted the emergency funds available to a surviving brother, whereas the loss of a sister was less financially detrimental to a surviving brother.

DISCUSSION

Recognizing that Baby Boomers will have as much or more opportunity to seek support from siblings as from children, we undertook this study of how sibling bereavements affect adults in late life. Our analyses are the first to quantify this phenomenon using population-based U.S. data. It includes a wide-range of health and psychosocial measures of well-being from a large biracial urban-rural sample.

The likelihood of sibling bereavement in this population was at least three times that of spousal bereavement (9 to 10% vs. 1.5 to 3%) and approximately one-third that of friendship bereavement (9 to 10% vs. 25 to 30%). One-half of elderly community-dwellers survived one year without experiencing any kin or non-kin bereavement.

Unexpectedly, bereaved siblings were more likely to evaluate their loss as positive than were any of the other bereaved groups. Whether this excess positive appraisal was due to self-interest (e.g., hope of inheritance or downward social comparison) or altruism (e.g., relief at the end of a family member's suffering) cannot be known from our data. We would have expected a strongly negative appraisal based on work by Hagestad [28]. Hagestad called the oldest living generation in a family the "Omega generation"—that which is closest to death. Grandparents and then parents usually fulfill this family role until a person's middle or late life. However, when both grandparents and parents are dead (as is the case in our sample), respondents and their siblings become members of the Omega generation themselves. When an elderly sibling dies, an individual feel his or her own mortality threatened. Even hostile siblings experience this threat when they and their siblings are in the Omega generation. For this reason, the excess positive appraisal of sibling deaths in our study is particularly puzzling.

Table 4. Differences in Health, Social, and Economic Resource Deficits across Bereavement Groups: Men

	Men: Bereavement Experience[a]							Significant Differences[b]
	Sibling		Spouse		Friend		None	
Characteristic	X̄(se)	%	X̄(se)	%	X̄(se)	%	X̄(se)	%	Sibs vs. Others[b]

Characteristic	X̄(se)	%	X̄(se)	%	X̄(se)	%	X̄(se)	%	Sibs vs. Others[b]
Health Deficits									
ADL deficits	0.58 (.11)		0.56 (.23)		0.24 (.05)		0.43 (.04)		Sibs > Fr
Nagi deficits	1.04 (.13)		0.82 (.26)		0.81 (.06)		0.75 (.05)		NS
Hospitalizations (past yr.)	0.31 (.09)		0.35 (.18)		0.38 (.04)		0.28 (.04)		NS
CESD score	1.64 (.33)		6.42 (.67)		2.51 (.15)		1.68 (.13)		Sibs < Sp/Fr
SPMSQ errors[c]	2.00 (.20)		1.53 (.41)		1.47 (.10)		1.94 (.08)		Sibs > Fr
Poor SRH[d]	2.56 (.09)		1.83 (.20)		2.31 (.04)		2.36 (.04)		Sibs > Sp/Fr
Life satisfaction	18.49 (.55)		16.01 (1.13)		19.06 (.26)		19.19 (.22)		NS
Social and Economic Deficits									
Perceived support	5.60 (.12)		4.95 (.25)		5.38 (.06)		5.39 (.05)		Sibs > Sp
Locus of control (internal)	3.92 (.19)		3.29 (.64)		4.00 (.10)		4.26 (.08)		NS
Enough $ for needs									NS
Poorly		9.1		2.6		11.2		12.3	
Fairly well		45.3		18.2		43.8		42.5	
Very well		45.6		80.2		45.0		45.2	
Enough $ for emergencies									NS
No		20.2		6.4		19.5		23.0	
Yes		79.8		93.6		80.5		77.0	

[a]All means are from 1989 adjusted for baseline scores from 1986 and age, except Locus of control which was not included in the baseline interview.
[b]Significant differences include pairwise differences in mean scores or proportions between sibling bereaved and any of the three comparison groups where $p \leq 0.0167$ (= 0.05 ÷ 3 comparisons).

The hypothesis that physical health problems would characterize sibling and spousal bereavement more than friend bereavement was largely supported. In general, the functional and cognitive status of surviving siblings was worse than that of surviving friends, underscoring the importance of family history with respect to health status. Whereas bereaved friends may share many of the same attributes (e.g., gender, geography, life style) as the friend who died, they do not share a genetic inheritance, and thus would not be expected to share a family history risk of specific diseases or more generalized frailty. Although there is an extensive literature documenting the excess morbidity and mortality following widowhood, our findings are the first to show no differences in specific health outcomes between spousal and sibling bereaved elders. However, the optimal comparison in this regard would be between bereaved siblings and non-bereaved siblings.

Contrary to our hypothesis, bereaved siblings discounted their overall health status to a greater extent than did bereaved spouses. Twenty years ago, Victor Marshall [29] suggested that individuals perform a "crude form of calculus" in estimating their own life expectancy, including an evaluation of the age to which siblings survived. Ellen Idler (personal communication, 1995) has surmised that some of the residual unexplained variance in overall self-ratings of health which remains when objective health predictors of overall health are controlled may be due to conscious or unconscious comparisons of the morbidity or mortality of kin and others in the social environment to that of the elderly respondent. Our findings support both of these hypotheses: overall self-ratings of health were demonstrably worse among bereaved siblings compared to bereaved spouses, as well as among bereaved brothers compared to men bereaved of friends. These differences persisted when functional and cognitive status as well as mood (for men) were controlled, suggesting that elders weight the death of kin very highly when calculating their overall health status.

The evidence for non-significant differences in mood and social support was mixed. On the one hand, loss of a spouse had a significantly more negative impact among men than did loss of a sibling: widowers reported significantly more mood and intimacy deficits than bereaved brothers. The experience of widows, on the other hand, was consonant with our hypothesis in that they reported similar levels of depressive symptoms, life satisfaction, and satisfaction with the availability of a confidante as other bereaved groups. It may be that for more specific separation distress measures (as opposed to a depressive symptom measures such as the CES-D) would have distinguished these groups of women. One group of bereaved women, i.e., sisters who lost brothers, showed a tendency toward greater distress than sisters who lost sisters. Although the reason for this is unclear, the finding is consonant with that of Cleiren's study of bereaved siblings in Holland [8].

Finally, the socioeconomic hypothesis was not supported in that recent widows and widowers reported the same patterns of financial need as did bereaved siblings and friends. In subanalyses, however, the loss of a brother reduced financial resources for the surviving brother when loss of a sister had no effect on a brother's finances. This may suggest that brothers are more fiscally co-mingled through "family businesses" or other enterprises, whereas sisters may be more likely to be financially intertwined with their husbands and perhaps the husband's family than with their own siblings. However, because the sample size of these particular subgroups was so small, conclusions based on our data are highly speculative and require testing in larger, more focused studies of bereaved siblings.

The non-bereaved group was not significantly different from the sibling bereaved group on any outcome measure; nor were outcome scores of the non-bereaved consistently better than scores of bereaved siblings. Mean outcome scores among the non-bereaved sometimes fell in the middle of the range of outcome scores reported by the bereavement groups and sometimes fell outside that range. It may be that the non-bereaved group was so heterogeneous that estimates of their relative risk were confounded in important ways by other uncontrollable variables. However, the consistently non-significant comparison with the other exposure groups is intriguing.

There are several limitations to our study, primarily with regard to measurement methods. First, because the report of sibling death is combined in the same interview item with all "other close (non-spouse, non-child) relatives," a true prevalence of sibling bereavement cannot be calculated. Sample members who were bereaved of a sibling as well as a parent, cousin, grandchild, or other relative were offered only a forced choice of a single kinship loss to report. Second, where a sibling death is reported, we do not know either the number or birth order of siblings in that generation of the respondent's family. Nor do we have even a proxy measure of sibling solidarity, e.g., geographical distance or perceived emotional intimacy. Such specific data would enhance the specificity of theory development and hypothesis testing. Finally, our interview instrument does not include a specific measure of separation distress or grief, such as the Texas Revised Inventory of Grief (TRIG) or the Jacobs Inventory of Loss-Related Distress (see [30] for a review) which might provide a much more sensitive assessment of psychosocial adaptation following all types of bereavement considered herein.

In summary, the functional, cognitive and subjective health of bereaved siblings appears to be worse than that of bereaved spouses or friends. However, bereaved spouses appear to suffer more from mood alterations and social support deficits than bereaved siblings. The impact of sibling deaths on socioeconomic factors appears to be limited to brothers of bereaved brothers. Hospice and other terminal care programs should alert surviving families of the excess risk of functional and cognitive deficits and of a worsening self-rating of health among siblings of the deceased, even where mood alterations and negative appraisal of

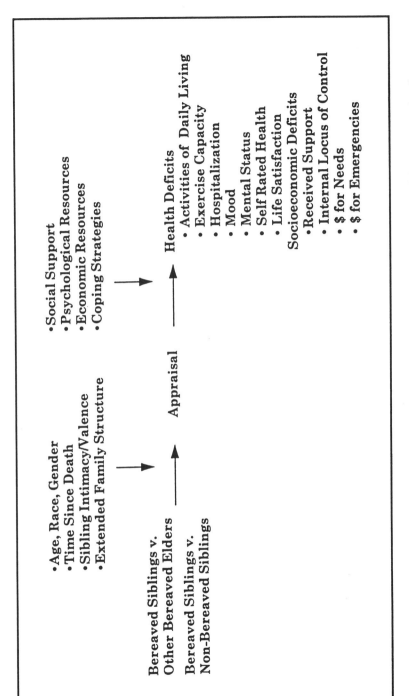

Figure 2. Hypothesized relationships among a stressful life event (bereavement), appraisal of the event, and various health-related and socioeconomic outcomes, as tested in the current study.

the loss and its social consequences are not apparent in the surviving sibling. As suggested in Figure 2, future research would benefit from additional measures of the pre-death intimacy and valence of the sibling relationship. Such data would permit comparisons of bereaved and non-bereaved siblings which was not possible with our data.

REFERENCES

1. M. M. Seltzer, The Three R's of Life Cycle Sibships: Rivalries, Reconstructions, and Relationships, *American Behavioral Scientist, 33*, pp. 107-115, 1989.
2. D. T. Gold, Continuities and Discontinuities in Sibling Relationships Across the Life Span, in *Adulthood and Aging: Research on Continuities and Discontinuities*, V. L. Bengtson (ed.), Springer, New York, in press.
3. I. A. Connidis, Siblings as Friends in Later Life, *American Behavioral Scientist, 33*, pp. 81-93, 1989.
4. D. T. Gold, Generational Solidarity: Conceptual Antecedents and Consequences, *American Behavioral Scientist, 33*, pp. 9-32, 1989.
5. S. Z. Moss and M. S. Moss, The Impact of the Death of an Elderly Sibling: Some Considerations of a Normative Loss, *American Behavioral Scientist, 33*, pp. 94-106, 1989.
6. G. L. Engel, The Death of a Twin: Mourning and Anniversary Reactions—Fragments of Ten Years of Self-Analysis, *International Journal of Psychoanalysis, 56*, pp. 23-40, 1975.
7. J. Holland, S. Harris, and J. Holmes, Psychological Responses to the Death of a Twin by the Surviving Twin with the Same Disease, *Omega: Journal of Death and Dying, 2*, pp. 160-167, 1971.
8. M. P. H. D. Cleiren, *Adaptation after Bereavement: A Comparative Study of the Aftermath of Death from Suicide, Traffic Accident and Illness for Next of Kin*, DSWO Press, Leiden University, Leiden, 1991.
9. H. G. Ross and J. I. Milgram, Important Variables in Adult Sibling Relationships: A Qualitative Study, in *Sibling Relationships: Their Nature and Significance across the Life Span*, M. E. Lamb and B. Sutton-Smith (eds.), Lawrence Erlbaum Associates, Hillsdale, New Jersey, pp. 225-249, 1982.
10. D. T. Gold, *Sibling Relationships in Retrospect: A Study of Reminiscence in Old Age*, unpublished doctoral dissertation, Northwestern University, Evanston, Illinois, 1986.
11. D. T. Gold, Siblings in Old Age: Something Special, *Canadian Journal of Aging, 6*, pp. 199-215, 1987.
12. D. T. Gold, Sibling Relationships in Old Age: A Typology, *International Journal of Aging and Human Development, 28*, pp. 37-51, 1989.
13. J. Bowlby, *The Making and Breaking of Affectional Bonds*, Tavistock Publications, London, 1979.

14. D. T. Gold, M. A. Woodbury, and L. K. George, Relationship Classification Using Grade of Membership (GOM) Analysis: A Typology of Sibling Relationships in Later Life, *Journal of Gerontology, 45*, pp. S43-S51, 1990.
15. D. T. Gold, Late-Life Sibling Relationships: Does Race Affect Typological Distribution? *The Gerontologist, 30*, pp. 741-748, 1990.
16. R. S. Weiss, Loss and Recovery, in *Handbook of Bereavement*, M. S. Stroebe, W. Stroebe, and R. O. Hansson (eds.), Cambridge University Press, Cambridge, pp. 271-284, 1993.
17. W. Stroebe and M. S. Stroebe, *Bereavement and Health: The Psychological and Physical Consequences of Partner Loss*, Cambridge University Press, Cambridge, 1987.
18. C. L. Ehlers, E. Frank, and D. J. Kupfer, Social Zeitgebers and Biological Rhythms: A Unified Approach to Understanding the Etiology of Depression, *Archives of General Psychiatry, 45*, pp. 948-952, 1988.
19. J. Cornoni-Huntley, D. G. Blazer, M. E. Lafferty, D. F. Everett, D. B. Brock, and M. E. Farmer (eds.), *Established Populations for the Epidemiologic Studies of the Elderly, Vol. II: Resource Data Book*, NIA Publication No. 90-945, National Institute on Aging, U.S. Dept. of Health and Human Services, Washington, D.C., 1990.
20. S. Katz and C. A. Akpom, A Measure of Primary Sociobiological Functions, *International Journal of Health Services, 6*, pp. 493-508, 1976.
21. S. Z. Nagi, An Epidemiology of Disability among Adults in the United States, *Milbank Memorial Fund Quarterly, 54*, pp. 439-467, 1976.
22. E. A. Pfeiffer, A Short Portable Mental Status Questionnaire for the Assessment of Organic Brain Deficit in Elderly Patients, *Journal of the American Geriatrics Society, 23*, pp. 433-441, 1975.
23. L. S. Radloff, The CES-D Scale: A Self-Reported Depression Scale for Research in the General Population, *Applied Psychological Measures, 1*, pp. 385-401, 1977.
24. J. C. Hays, D. S. Schoenfeld, and D. G. Blazer, Determinants of Poor Self-Rated Health in Late Life, *American Journal of Geriatric Psychiatry, 4*, pp. 188-196.
25. B. Neugarten, R. J. Havighurst, and S. S. Tobin. The Measurement of Life Satisfaction, *Journal of Gerontology, 16*, pp. 134-143, 1961.
26. J. B. Rotter, Generalized Expectancies for Internal vs. External Control of Reinforcement, *Psychological Monographs, 80*, 1966.
27. R. Landerman, L. K. George, R. T. Campbell, and D. G. Blazer, Social Support, Stress and Depression: Alternative Models of the Stress Buffering Hypothesis, *American Journal of Community Psychology, 17*, pp. 625-642, 1989.
28. G. O. Hagestad, The Continuous Bond: A Dynamic, Multigenerational Perspective on Parent-Child Relations between Adults, in *Parent-Child Interactions and Parent-Child Relations in Child Development*, M. Perlmutter (ed.), The Minnesota Symposium on Child Psychology, Vol. 17, Erlbaum, Hillsdale, New Jersey, pp. 129-158, 1984.
29. V. Marshall, Age and Awareness of Finitude in Developmental Gerontology, *Omega: Journal of Death and Dying, 6*, pp. 113-129, 1975.

30. S. Jacobs, Measures of the Psychological Distress of Bereavement, in *Biopsychosocial Dimensions of Bereavement*, S. Zisook (ed.), APA Press, Washington, D.C., pp. 139-155, 1987.

THE ROLE OF GENDER IN MIDDLE-AGE CHILDREN'S RESPONSES TO PARENT DEATH*

MIRIAM S. MOSS

NANCY RESCH

SIDNEY Z. MOSS

Philadelphia Geriatric Center

ABSTRACT

The impact of the deaths of the last surviving elderly parent of 212 middle-aged children was studied. Daughters expressed more emotional upset, somatic response, and continuing tie with the deceased parent than sons; sons reported more acceptance of the death than daughters. The child's gender was not associated with a sense of personal finitude or control of grief. When we control in regressions for characteristics of the parent, the child, and the quality of their relationship, child's gender continued to add significantly to the bereavement outcomes above.

This article examines gender differences in bereavement, and explores how these gender differences are expressed by middle-aged sons and daughters after the death of their last surviving parent.

There is a tendency for bereavement research to focus primarily on mental health (e.g., depression) and changes in physical health [1, 2]. Although these are significant areas they tend to mask rather than to encompass the wide range of themes that occur in bereavement. This research reflects three additional basic

---

*This research is funded by National Institute on Aging, Grant R01-AG10875, Children's Perspective on Death of an Elderly Parent, Robert L. Rubinstein, P.I.

© 1997, Baywood Publishing Co., Inc.

themes which are central to our conceptualization of bereavement as a process and not an event.

1. *The process of bereavement involves strong cognitive, as well as behavioral and emotional components.* There are multiple cognitive shifts in the way the bereaved person views the deceased, the self and the world [3-5]. Two shifts are in acceptance and finitude. Acceptance begins with the recognition that the death has occurred and continues as part of the complex process of integrating the meaning of that irrevocable fact into the life and world view of the survivor. A second cognitive shift involves personal finitude—an increased awareness that the future is foreshortened and one is nearer to one's own death [6].

2. *Bereavement is an active process* in which people modify their behavior, particularly in social contexts [7]. Rather than bereavement being viewed as a passive condition, it involves continuous choices and strategies. One example is in the area of control of the expression of grief. Survivors repeatedly monitor their behavior and make decisions about how they wish to appear to themselves and to others.

3. *Close attachments in life are not severed after death.* The ties that bind living kin continue to be viable over the lifetime [8]. Middle-aged persons whose parents have died may continue to find comfort and solace in thoughts and memories of parents thus maintaining a meaningful bond. They may often project their tie into the future, anticipating that they will be reunited with their parent again [9].

SIGNIFICANCE OF THE STUDY

The death of a loved one is considered a major human loss. Although untimely death of children or young adults are particularly difficult to bear, family losses that are considered on time and normative also have considerable impact on surviving kin. For example, the death of an elderly spouse may evoke shifts in personal identity, and quality of family relationships as well as persistent feelings of loneliness, and difficulties in dealing with unfamiliar tasks of daily living [10].

There are several areas of significance of research on the impact of parent death. First is the increasing prevalence and normalcy of parental loss in adulthood. Parents are expected to die before their children, and anticipatory orphanhood may occur for many, as they recognize that someday they will continue to live after their parents have died [11]. When parents reach old age their death tends to become an on time family loss. For middle-aged children the loss may trigger a normative transition from being a child with living parents to being a child without living parents. Winsborough [12] suggests that the timing of a normative life-cycle transition begins when 25 percent of its members have experienced it and is completed when 75 percent of its members have experienced it. He found that for the 1920s birth cohort, the two middle quartiles of women had faced their mothers' death between ages thirty-five and fifty-nine (a period of 24 years). For the 1970 cohort, he predicts that half of the women will have a mother die when the daughters are between the ages of forty-nine and sixty-four (a period of only 15 years). As these figures suggest, there is a trend for parent death to occur later in the lifespan, and over a more compressed period of years. The death deserves increased attention as a midlife issue.

Second, death of a parent potentially may offer a model to understand death in old age. Almost three-quarters of all deaths in the United States are of persons over sixty-five years old [13]. About 80 percent of all persons age sixty-five and older have at least one living child. This may approximate the proportion of older people who die having a surviving child. Although most of the theory and research on bereavement has focused on widowhood of younger persons, and some on bereavement and death of young children, death of an elderly parent may be the most normative and on time family death. Studies of death of elderly parents have the potential to increase our understanding of bereavement for other kin, such as sibling and grandparent as well as spouse.

Third, the child's tie with the parent is unique in the life of a child. The bond is a phenomenon spanning the total life course. It begins in infancy when parenting involves protection, nurturance, guidance, and affection [14]. Much of the child's identity develops over decades of sharing life with parents. In middle age the child-parent bond is also multidimensional still carrying some aspects of earlier themes, as well as strong elements of independence and interdependence. The life of an old parent continues to be highly significant for children in middle age. Our earlier conceptualizations and research on parent death have indicated that the death does not sever the parent-child tie [9, 11, 15, 16]. Research on the meaning of the loss can increase our understanding of the meaning of the relationship in later years.

Fourth, and central to this article, the research provides the opportunity to examine how men and women are similar and different in their response to loss and bereavement. Much of the framework of bereavement theory is deeply rooted in clinical and research work with women who have experienced widowhood (e.g., [17]). Our previous research on this topic focused solely on daughters of mothers. In our earlier qualitative interviews, daughters often contrasted their own experience of bereavement with that of their brothers. The current research gives us the opportunity to look at gendered responses, potentially suggesting additional themes that can be applicable to other types of family losses.

Overall, the goal of the present analysis is to examine the personal meaning and experience of an elderly parent's death for sons and daughters. We will explore the ways that characteristics of the parent, characteristics of the child, and the quality of their relationship are associated with a range of bereavement outcomes.

BACKGROUND

Gender is a social construction, and is imbedded in cultural norms. The more a person is socialized to traditional gender norms, the more behaviors, attitudes, and emotional expression will reflect gender [18, 19].

In planning this study we had anticipated that sons and daughters would differ in their experience of and meaning of parent death. This expectation was based on four areas of research which examine differences between men and women: in their view of social relationships, in the ways that members of gendered parent-child dyads relate to each other, in the ways men and women respond to emotional upset and bereavement, including ways that the sons and daughters differ in the multiple dimensions of bereavement.

Some research has found that women's view of themselves is more highly imbedded in their relationships with others than men's [20, 21]. Women tend to value expressing and sharing their emotions more than men [18, 22]. On the other hand, men tend to be more individualistic, more private, more active, and more in control of their expression of emotions [23]. Thus, we may expect that daughters whose parent has died would express more emotional upset and maintain a stronger tie with the deceased parent than sons. Sons emphasizing a cognitive response might be more accepting of the social loss and more actively involved in controlling expression of their grief.

Research on the quality of the relationship between parents and their adult children has found that gender plays an important role. Overall, studies demonstrate more intense affectional ties between daughters and mothers than between members of the other three dyads. Conversely, the father-son relationship tends to be more conflictual, with the cross-gender dyads showing intermediate levels of closeness and conflict. Daughters and mothers tend to be more active in maintaining the tie than sons and fathers [24, 25]. From the perspective of the parents, mothers report more closeness with daughters than with sons [26], and see daughters more as confidants than sons [27]. Fathers report more closeness with their daughters than with their sons [26, 27]. Different dyads emphasize different aspects of the relationship, e.g., father-child more based on instrumental and obligatory themes, mother-child more on affection and personal affinity [28]. The children's perspectives are congruent with the parents. Daughters remain closer with more intimacy to both parents than sons and they feel closer to their mother than their father [26]. If the meaning of the parent-child relationship differs for sons and daughters, we might expect that the meaning of the death of a parent would also differ. In light of the above we anticipate that daughters of mothers would be more affected by the death, showing more emotional upset and more somatic problems, and feeling more closely tied to mother than children of other dyads. Further, that sons of fathers would be more accepting of the death, controlling their expression of feelings more, and having less grief than other dyads.

Men and women tend to have somewhat different patterns of emotional expressions and reactions to bereavement. Overall, women tend to have higher rates of depression and anxiety, two major emotional responses to stressful situations [29]. There is some evidence that men tend to be less affected emotionally by life events [30].

Research has suggested that the meaning of the loss and the world of the bereaved have both similarities and differences for men and women [1, 31]. Some have reported that widows have greater distress and depression than widowers [32] while others have found that widowers have greater difficulty (higher risk of mortality, more loss of social support) [33]. Lund et al., however, found that widows and widowers (age 50+) did not differ in their emotional, psychological, health, and social adjustments [34]. Overall, there is increasing evidence that widowhood may have different meanings for men and women; widowhood may not be the same event for the two genders [5]. This is reflected in differences in vulnerabilities of widowed men (e.g., in social relationships and taking on female tasks) vis-à-vis widowed women (e.g., in financial strain) [35].

Arbuckle and de Vries reported that gender exerted an influence on four major outcomes in their model of bereavement for widows and surviving parents all over age fifty-five [36]. In their study bereaved men were higher in self-efficacy (analogous to our measure of mastery) than women. On the other hand, women were higher in depression than men, and their views of the world involved more fatalism and more personal vulnerability. Littlewood [37] studying parents of young children who had died found that women tended to use passive methods of coping (such as social support and emotional expression) while men preferred more active coping (involving problem solving and tension reduction).

Previous research on the impact of parent death on sons vis-à-vis daughters has been sparse. A major study of young children (ages 6 to 17) found that the child's gender was not associated with affective responses or behavioral problems, nor was gender of the parent associated with major differences in children's affective responses [38]. Girls however, were more likely than boys to share their feelings about the death with family and friends.

Some studies of adults whose parents have recently died have reported no gender differences in depression [39], or in grief at the time of the interview [40]. On the other hand, there is some evidence that daughters have a harder time adjusting to the death [39]. Scharlach [40] reports that daughters of fathers had a stronger initial reaction to the death than son's of fathers, while Umberson [39] reported that the death of a mother led to more depression than the death of a father. The child's lack of autonomy from the parent has been found to be associated with more upset after parent death [41], but little research has examined the relationship between the quality of the parent-child tie and the subsequent reaction to the parent's death.

METHOD

The Measures

Although the primary focus of this article is on the role of the bereaved adult child's gender in response to the parent's death, we also will examine other characteristics which theory and previous research suggest are potentially important. The perceived characteristics of the deceased person may be expected to play a role in family members' reactions. If the parent had been frail and dependent on others for daily care, the child may have been more likely to anticipate the approach of death. Much literature suggests that sudden, unexpected deaths have considerable impact [42]. The loss of a parent who appears closer to death may have less effect on the surviving child than the death of a parent who is functioning independently.

Characteristics of the child may also play a role in the outcome. Background characteristics as well as psychosocial attributes potentially may have some impact on bereavement outcomes. Finally, the quality of the relationship between the parent and child is a factor to consider.

Thus, four groups of measures are examined here: the parent's characteristics in the final year, the child's characteristics, the quality of the parent-child tie, and bereavement measures. Table 1 summarizes the number of items and alpha reliability of each measure.

Parent Characteristics

The parent's characteristics include gender, age at death, years since the death of the first parent, functioning in activities of daily living (ADL), cognitive functioning, quality of life, intensity of terminal care, and three contexts of the last part of life. Each was reported or judged by the child. All parents were living within an hour's drive of the child. ADL functioning (alpha = .96) is measured by the sum of months in the final year that the parent was able independently to carry out each of eleven activities of daily living (e.g., feeding, bathing, dressing, shopping, laundry, housework). Cognitive functioning is the sum of ratings of memory for two segments of the final year: the first nine months and the last three months. Quality of life (alpha = .81) equals the number of high quality of life areas for the same two time segments of the final year for: a fair amount of pep and energy, infrequent pain, seldom depressed, satisfaction with time use, and interest in the world [43]. Intensity of terminal care (alpha = .79) is a sum of standard scores of five measures of duration of hospitalization, intensive care, being on a respirator, having intervenous or other tubes, or being cared for in a coma. Also, three contexts of the parents' last year of life were dummy coded: nursing home residence (for at least the final 3 months), recipient of heavy caregiving for at least three months while coresident with the child (helped with at least 2 personal self-care activities such as feeding, bathing, dressing), and relatively independent parents.

Child Characteristics

Background characteristics include gender, age, race, religion (3 dummy codes of Protestant, Catholic, Jewish), and socioeconomic status (SES, alpha = .75, which is the sum of standard scores of education, occupation, and household income). In addition to background characteristics we measured the child's health and personal mastery. Self-rated health was measured by a single standard item: Would you say that your health in general is: excellent, very good, good, fair, poor? Personal mastery, a major resource in coping with threatening events [44] represents the degree to which one sees life as being under one's own control rather than the control of others or chance. The seven-item scale has an alpha reliability = .80 for this sample. Positive affect was measured by the five items which tap positive affect in the Bradburn Affect Balance Scale [45] with an alpha in this study = .76. A list of eleven life events in the prior year related to paid work, family, illness, and other deaths. These were obtained to place the parent's death within the context of other potentially significant occurrences in the respondent's life.

Quality of Parent-Child Relationship

Two indices of the relationship are overall quality and guilt. The global quality of the relationship (3 items, alpha = .94) was measured as in previous research [9]. Items included: Overall, what would you say was the *quality* of your relationship with your (parent)? (Excellent, good, fair, poor). Taking everything into consideration, how close do you feel the relationship was between you and your (parent)? (Extremely close, very close, somewhat close, not at all close). Guilt (alpha = .89) represents children's feelings that they did not help the parent as much or spend as much time with the parent as they should have. An example of one of the four items: No matter how much I did, somehow I felt guilty about not doing enough for my (parent).

Bereavement Outcomes

Six bereavement outcomes were developed in our research on parent death, four in a previous all-female study sample [9], and two for this study. Unless otherwise noted each of the items was rated by the respondents on a 4-point or 5-point Likert scale.

GRIEF is a composite of twelve items (alpha = .92). The focus of the GRIEF index is the emotional response to the death including a theme of loneliness. Items include: I still cry when I think of my (parent). Losing a parent is one of the hardest things I've had to deal with. Overall, considering everything, how much sorrow or grief have you experienced over your (parent's) death? Seven of the items are part of the Texas Revised Inventory of Grief (TRIG) [46] which

Table 1. Characteristics of Total Sample and Dyads

	No. Items	Alpha	Overall Mean	Daughters of: Mothers $n=65$ (1)	Daughters of: Fathers $n=53$ (2)	Sons of: Mothers $n=53$ (3)	Sons of: Fathers $n=41$ (4)	F	Dyad Difference	t-Tests
Parent										
Age	1		81.2	82.1	78.4	82.6	81.3	3.20*	3 > 2	MO > FA*
ADL independence	11	.96	61.4	—	—	—	—	n.s.		FA > MO*
Cognitive functioning	2		4.8	—	—	—	—	n.s.		
Quality of life	10	.81	4.6	—	—	—	—	n.s.		
Intensity of terminal care	5	.79	.25	—	—	—	—	n.s.		
Yrs between parent deaths	1		14.9	20.1	10.1	14.4	13.8	6.84***	1 > 2	MO > FA***
Adult child										
Age	1		52.2	54.6	48.7	54.2	50.3	7.24***	1>2,4,3>2	MO > FA***
Socioeconomic status	3	.75	-.03	-.86	-.81	1.11	.86	13.99***	3,4 > 1,2	SO > DA***
Catholic	1		40.6%	—	—	—	—	n.s.		
Protestant	1		36.8%	—	—	—	—	n.s.		
Jewish	1		15.6%	—	—	—	—	n.s.		
African American	1		24.0%	—	—	—	—	n.s.		
Currently married	1		80.0%	—	—	—	—	n.s.		
Subjective health	1		7.8	7.6	7.4	8.4	8.1	3.34*	3 > 2	SO > DA**
Personal mastery	7	.75	26.8	25.9	25.3	28.6	27.9	4.16**	3 > 1,2	SO > DA***
Positive affect	5	.76	3.5	—	—	—	—	n.s.		
Recent life events	11		2.1	—	—	—	—	n.s.		

Parent-child relationship									
Global quality	3	.92	9.8	9.9	10.3	9.9	8.9	2.99*	2 > 4	—
Guilt	4	.88	9.5	8.0	9.9	10.2	10.5	2.82*	—	SO > DA*
Bereavement outcomes									
Grief	12	.92	38.7	41.8	44.6	32.9	33.4	18.79***	1,2 > 3,4	DA > SO***
Somatic	6	.72	1.3	1.8	1.9	0.5	0.7	14.46***	1,2 > 3,4	DA > SO***
Acceptance	8	.79	29.8	29.2	26.9	31.7	32.1	8.70***	3,4 > 2	SO > DA***
Finitude	5	.77	12.2	—	—	—	—	n.s.		FA > MO*
Tie with deceased parent	14	.90	42.2	46.1	45.6	37.7	37.3	16.31***	1,2 > 3,4	DA > SO***
Control of grief	6	.74	14.0	—	—	—	—	n.s.		

*p ≤ .05
**p ≤ .01
***p ≤ .001

measures current grief. Thus the correlation with the TRIG is very high ($r = .93$). We selected GRIEF as our measure instead of the current TRIG because we found that three other outcome measures (ACCEPTANCE, TIE, and CONTROL) were strengthened by several TRIG items. Although the current TRIG had a very high alpha (= .88) in this study sample, we found that it includes items in our multiple dimensions that can benefit from separate analyses.

The SOMATIC measure is a composite of changes in health or health-related practices since parent's death (each was a dichotomy). These include worsened health problems, insomnia, weight change, use of psychotropic medication, (6 items, alpha = .72).

The third measure, ACCEPTANCE, represents a sense of timeliness and of fairness of the death, and ability to see oneself as living on without a parent (8 items, alpha = .79). Items include: It was a blessing that my (parent) died when s/he did. When someone lives as long as my (parent) did, it's not really a tragedy when they die. I feel I'm able to plan my future without my (parent). I cannot accept my (parent's) death (reflected) (a TRIG item). I feel that it's unfair that my (parent) died. (A TRIG item.)

A fourth measure, FINITUDE focuses on an increasing sense of closeness to one's own death [47] with a perception of a shortened personal future (5 items, alpha = .77). Items include: Since my (parent's) death I feel I am closer to death. Since my (parent) died my future seems to be shorter.

The above four measures were developed in our earlier research [9]. The remaining two outcome measures were developed for this study.

TIE, a measure of the degree to which the child continues to be connected with the deceased parent was expanded conceptually from our previous research [9]. It is a composite of fourteen items which represent symbolic ties with the parent through memory and thought, as well as more active ties to the parent such as doing things that the parent had expected (alpha = .90). This index includes: I am preoccupied with thoughts (or often think) about (parent) (a TRIG item). Things and people around me still remind me of my (parent) (a TRIG item). I feel s/he is with me at times. I still talk to or communicate with my (parent). I am interested in carrying out his/her work or wishes. I think I will be with my (parent) again some day.

Finally, as a result of qualitative analyses in our earlier study we recognized the salience of the control of grief [see 15]. CONTROL is a measure of the degree to which the child regulates feelings or expressions of sadness and upset over the death, or the context in which these feelings are expressed. The six items (alpha = .73) include: I hide my tears when I think of my (parent) (a TRIG item). I don't want to look weak in the way I respond to my (parent's) death. In some ways I have controlled the way I have felt about my (parent's) death. I want to protect others from my sad feelings about my (parent's) death.

The Sample

The sample included 212 children whose last surviving parent, age sixty-five or over, had died within the previous six to ten months. Participants were selected randomly from death certificates in Philadelphia county. Each of the respondents was between forty and sixty-five years of age, and was currently married or living with an adult. Although the design called for approximately equal representation of the four dyads: daughter of mother (DAMO), daughter of father (DAFA), son of mother (SOMO), and son of father (SOFA), the actual numbers attained range from forty-one (SOFA) to sixty-five (DAMO). Within each dyad we sought to represent parents who had lived in a nursing home, had received heavy caregiving, as well as those who had lived relatively independently.

Lengthy tape recorded qualitative interviews (lasting an average of just under two hours) were generally held in the respondent's home. After each interview ended the participant was asked to complete a twenty-page self-administered, structured questionnaire and mail it in to the research office. Over 97 percent of the respondents returned fully completed questionnaires, and these are the focus of this article.

Table 1, column 1 highlights the background characteristics of the 212 participants. Overall, 44 percent were sons and 56 percent were daughters. Their average age was 52.5. Eighty percent were currently married. The parent's average age was 81.1. Respondents had a wide range of formal education (mean 14 years), income (mean $42,000). Twenty-four percent were African American, the remainder Caucasian. Their religious identification was diverse: 41 percent Catholic, 37 percent Protestant, and 16 percent Jewish. The death of the first parent had occurred an average of fifteen years prior to the death of this, the last parent.

FINDINGS

All differences between sons and daughters were substantiated by t tests, or chi square as appropriate. One way ANOVAs compared the four dyads (DAMO, DAFA, SOMO, SOFA) on each of the measures. We present one-way ANOVAs findings rather than two-way ANOVAs because they clearly delineate the dyad similarities and differences. Here, as elsewhere in the article, we will report only findings that reach the .05 level of significance. There are both strong similarities and substantial differences between dyads, particularly between sons and daughters.

GENDER SIMILARITIES AND DIFFERENCES

Characteristics of the Parents

The parents differed in expected ways. Deceased mothers were older (82.3) than deceased fathers (79.7), ($t = 2.49$, $p < .05$), and mothers of daughters were significantly older than fathers of daughters. There were more years separating the parents' deaths for mothers (17.5 years) than fathers (11.5 years) ($t = 3.39$, $p < .001$), and more for DAMOs than DAFAs. Fathers had greater ADL independence in their final year than mothers, although there were no dyad differences ($t = -2.03$, $p < .05$). Parents, however, did not differ in their level of cognitive functioning in the final year, their quality of life, or the intensity of their terminal care.

Characteristics of the Children

Some background characteristics of the children such as religious identification, race, and marital status were similar across the dyads. We did find some expected demographic differences: children of deceased mothers were older (54.4) than children of fathers (49.4) ($t = 4.56$, $p < .001$). The socioeconomic status of sons was consistently higher than that of daughters ($t = -6.30$, $p < .001$), reflecting sons' higher education, occupation, and household income. The subjective health of sons was higher than that of daughters ($t = -3.14$, $p < .002$). SOMOs had better health than DAFAs.

Sons and daughters, and individual dyads did not differ in the number of life events they experienced in the last year. There were also no differences in positive affect. There were however, clear dissimilarities in personal mastery. Sons reported higher levels of personal mastery than daughters ($t = -3.45$, $p < .001$), with SOMOs higher in mastery than daughters of either parent.

Quality of Parent-Child Tie

Although the functioning of their parents over the final year is quite similar for daughters and sons, other analyses indicate that daughters helped their parent with twice as many tasks as sons (5.0 vs. 2.7 tasks). This may reflect the overall tendency of women to carry primary responsibility for family caregiving. Sons expressed greater guilt about caregiving than daughters ($t = -2.12$, $p < .05$). This was particularly reflected in the tendency of sons more than daughters to feel they should have spent more time with their parent. Although there was no significant difference between sons and daughters in the overall quality of their relationship with their parents, DAFAs reported higher global quality than SOFAs.

Bereavement Outcomes

Daughters express more GRIEF ($t = 7.34$, $p < .001$), report more SOMATIC symptoms ($t = 6.89$, $p < .001$), and have a stronger TIE with their deceased parent than sons ($t = 7.01$, $p < .001$). Sons, on the other hand have more ACCEPTANCE of their parent's death ($t = -4.73$, $p < .001$). All sons have greater ACCEPTANCE than DAFAs. Sons particularly see the death as less of a tragedy and less unfair. Sons and daughters did not differ in their feelings of personal FINITUDE, rather children of fathers had greater sense of finitude than children of mothers. There were no differences at all in CONTROL of grief.

ROLE OF CHILD'S GENDER IN EXPLAINING BEREAVEMENT OUTCOMES

As discussed previously our concern with bereavement goes beyond the emotional sadness or upset in GRIEF, or the impact on the surviving child's health (SOMATIC). In addition we are concerned with the impact on the sense of self (FINITUDE), the degree of ACCEPTANCE of the death, the extent to which the TIE with the dead parent continues, and the active stance of the CONTROL of grief.

Using hierarchical multiple regression, we examine these six bereavement outcomes separately, in order to ascertain the degree to which the characteristics of the elder, the child, and their relationship explain the variance of each outcome. The specific items selected were those with significant bivariate correlations with the outcomes as well as variables of interest in the light of previous theory and research. We included two contexts of the parents' final year (having lived in a nursing home and having received heavy care giving from the child) because in our previous research these had been found to be significantly associated with bereavement outcomes [9]. The comparison group not in the equation was parents who were living independently most of their final year. All of the above variables were entered in the first step of the regression. The child's gender was entered in the second step to see whether it adds to our understanding of each outcome. Additionally, we did explore the parent's gender and the interaction between parent's and child's gender. These were never significant in these regression equations, and thus they are not presented here.

The zero-order correlations between each of the outcomes and the variables in the model are presented in Table 2. These bivariate associations are not discussed separately here, but they will be referred to throughout our discussion of the regression equations. Specifically we will delineate where strong bivariate associations do exist, although they are not sufficiently unique to be significant in the multivariate analysis.

For each bereavement outcome Table 3 presents the standardized regression weights (betas) for the model excluding (model I) and including (model II) the

Table 2. Correlations between Bereavement Outcomes and Variables in the Model

	Grief	Somatic	Accept	Finitude	Tie	Control
Characteristics of parent						
ADL independence	.15*		–.17*	.19**		
Cognitive functioning	.17*		–.24***		.16*	
Quality of life	.19**		–.30***		.26***	
In nursing home	–.38**	–.17*	.34***	–.23***	–.35***	–.18**
Received heavy care	.21**	.20**			.25***	.14*
Characteristics of child						
Age	–.21**		.29***		–.14*	
Socioeconomic status	–.36***	–.31***	.36***		–.36***	
Personal mastery	–.21**	–.32***	.21**	–.23***	–.15*	–.20**
Parent-child relationship						
Global quality	.44***	.15*	.30***		.53***	
Guilt				.30***		.35***
Child's gender (male)	–.45***	–.41***	.30***		–.44***	
Parent's gender (male)				.15*		

Correlations with two-tailed *p*-values ≤ .05 are listed.
*$p \leq .05$
**$p \leq .01$
***$p \leq .001$

child's gender. As Table 3 indicates prior to the entry of child's gender more intense GRIEF is associated with the parent not having lived in a nursing home, the child's younger age, lower SES, less personal mastery, and more positive quality of the parent-child relationship ($R^2 = .39$). The inclusion of gender (being a daughter) significantly increased the amount of variance explained (to $R^2 = .50$). We see that when gender was added the model changed: SES and mastery dropped out, and guilt entered the equation. A number of other variables had significant bivariate correlations with GRIEF (see Table 2) but none of these variables added a unique piece of variance to either regression equation; they include the parent's greater ADL independence, higher cognitive functioning, higher quality of life, and being a recipient of heavy caregiving.

SOMATIC problems were associated with the child's lower SES and lower sense of personal mastery ($R^2 = .19$). Again being a daughter explained a significant additional piece of variance of somatic difficulties ($R^2 = .27$). SES dropped out when gender entered the equation. We note that several variables that were significantly correlated with SOMATIC added no additional variance to the final equation. These include receiving heavy caregiving, not living in a nursing home, as well as a higher quality of the parent-child tie.

Greater ACCEPTANCE is explained by the parent's having lived in a nursing home or having received heavy caregiving from the child, and by the child's older age, and higher socioeconomic status, greater personal mastery, as well as poorer quality of parent-child tie ($R^2 = .36$). Gender of the child adds an additional piece of explained variance ($R^2 = .38$): being a son is associated with ACCEPTANCE. With the inclusion of gender in the model, personal mastery drops out and the contribution of parent's quality of life attains significance. Again, variables which had significant bivariate correlations with ACCEPTANCE did not enter into the equation, specifically parents with lower ADL and lower cognitive functioning.

A higher sense of personal FINITUDE—our major measure of impact on self—is explained by the parent's lower quality of life and having lived in a nursing home, and the child's higher SES, lower sense of mastery and greater guilt ($R^2 = .22$). The gender of the child did not add significantly to the model. Only one variable, higher ADL functioning of the parent, had a significant bivariate, correlation with FINITUDE yet did not enter into the equation.

The TIE with the deceased is stronger when the parent had not lived in a nursing home, the child's SES was lower, and the parent-child tie had been positive ($R^2 = .40$). The gender of the child—being a daughter—adds a significant piece of explained variance of ($R^2 = .49$). When gender entered the equation, SES dropped out. Several variables in the model had a significant bivariate correlation with TIE, but were not in either equation: parent's better memory, higher quality of life, receiving heavy caregiving, and the child's lower personal mastery.

The final regression models examined the CONTROL of grief. Our model explains less variance for this bereavement outcome than for any of the others. Significant in both equations are the parent not having lived in a nursing home, and the child feeling less mastery and more guilt. The child's gender explains no additional variance. Although having received heavy caregiving was significantly correlated on a bivariate level, it added nothing to the multivariate equation.

DISCUSSION

In comparing the four dyads of parent and child, with few exceptions, we found that major differences occurred between sons and daughters. Sons tend to differ from daughters in that they have more resources (higher SES). They tend to feel more guilt in relation to being with and caring for their parent. As we expected, sons express a greater sense of personal mastery, and are more accepting of their parent's death, and on the other hand they have less grief, fewer somatic difficulties, and less strong ties with their parent. This pattern reflects the male style of coping with bereavement in general which tends to be more stoic and less

Table 3. Regression Models for Bereavement Outcomes

MODEL:	Grief I	Grief II	Somatic I	Somatic II	Accept I	Accept II	Finitude I	Finitude II	Tie I	Tie II	Control I	Control II
Characteristics of parent												
ADL independence												
Cognitive functioning												
Quality of life												
In nursing home	-.23**	-.21**			.25**	.23**	-.17*	-.17*	-.21**	-.19**		
Received heavy care					.19*	.18*	-.21*	-.21*			.16*	.16*
Characteristics of child												
Age	-.15**				.13*	-.15*						
Socioeconomic status	-.19**		-.17*		.23**	.22***	.19**	.22**				
Personal mastery	-.13*	-.13*	-.26***	-.22**	.26***	.20**	-.23***	-.22**	-.18**		-.15*	-.15*
Parent child relationship												
Global quality	.41***	.40***			-.16*	-.15*	.27***	.28***	.47***	.45***	.35***	.35***
Guilt		.17**										
R^2 without child's gender in model (Model I)	.39		.19		.36		.22		.40		.19	
Child's gender (hi = male)		-.36***		-.31***		.17**				-.33***		
R^2 with child's gender in model (Model II)		.50		.27		.38		.23		.49		.19

Note: Entries are significant standardized betas.
*$p \leq .05$; **$p \leq .01$; ***$p \leq .001$

expressive, with more emphasis on privacy and less on relationships with and dependency on others. The overall salience of personal mastery for sons may enhance their adaptation, and play a role in determining their style of bereavement.

Daughters, being more rooted in social relationships maintain a stronger tie with their deceased parent than sons. Additionally, the daughter's greater expressiveness of emotional upset in grief is consonant with women's general tendency to report more depression and grief in the wake of family losses.

The DAFA dyad is distinctive from other dyads in a number of ways, which is not true of DAMOs. The DAFAs have poorer subjective health than SOMOs, they have better quality of relationship with their parent than SOFAs, and they are less accepting of the death than sons of either parent. In other analyses not reported here daughters were significantly more depressed than sons of either parent. There were no significant differences setting the DAFAs apart in other areas. Our observation that they do have the lowest mean score on mastery, highest on grief, highest on somatic difficulties, and the lowest score on acceptance of the death is suggestive for future research. The quality of the relationship between daughters and their fathers may be unique in some ways that influence the bereavement process.

Overall we have found that the gender of the adult child is associated with the way in which the child responds to the death of an elderly parent. When we control for a range of characteristics of the elder, of the child, and of their relationship we still find that daughters express considerably more emotional upset, more somatic symptoms since the parent's death, and have a stronger tie with the deceased parent, and sons are more accepting. These findings are congruent with our expectations. Bower (in this issue) throws considerable light on themes in acceptance of parent's death. In other linguistic analyses of our qualitative data, Bower found that sons saw acceptance more in terms of a factual, orderly experience, as part of the natural order of life, often resulting from physical decline. Daughters, while also accepting the physical fact of death, emphasize emotional components of their experience and often see the death as a reflection of God's will [48].

The few areas where parent gender was salient primarily reflect the tendency of fathers to die at a younger age than mothers. Thus, there were fewer years separating parent deaths when mothers predeceased fathers than in the more normative situation when fathers predeceased mothers. Although the differences were significant, overall there were few parent deaths which occurred in close proximity, only 12 percent died less than three years apart. Future analyses examining the impact of proximate parent deaths may help us to explore the meaning of sequential family losses. The other area where parent gender is important is in relation to finitude (see below).

We had expected that sons, relying more on doing and action, would report greater control over their grief than daughters, but we found no gender differences in control. Further analyses also did not show any interaction effects: there is evidence that control is greater when grief is greater at the bivariate level, and this was true for both sons and daughters. In a supplementary analysis not presented on Table 3, when we added GRIEF to the equation, we found that GRIEF explained a significant additional piece of variance of CONTROL ($R^2 = .25$). We might expect that more control of grief would result in the decrease in the expression of emotional upset after parent death, but it may be that more grief tends to engender more control. The relationship between grief and control suggests that there is an interactive process that continues over time. Immediately after the death, children often were willing to accept the initial burst of feeling seeing it as a necessary catharsis, but subsequently they reported guarding against expressions of grief. Intense expressions over time evoked further attempts at control.

Qualitative analyses of our lengthy interviews by Moss and Rubinstein add to our understanding of the apparent lack of difference in control of grief between sons and daughters [49]. They suggest that both sons and daughters use control of the expression of their feelings, but the meaning of the control is different: men control through modeling, women control through empathy. They found that sons, feeling that emotions hinder necessary action, tend to control their feelings in order to be strong and stoic offering a model to encourage others in the family to control their emotions as well. Daughters on the other hand, with their strong sense of empathy and connection with kin tend to control their feelings in order not to burden others.

A sense of personal finitude is a complex emotional and cognitive response to the death. Respondents were often speaking as new members of the Omega generation following the death of their last parent. Although the possibility of their death became more real to them, they resisted feeling that they were actually closer to death. Qualitative interviews suggest that many sons and daughters made it clear that they did not want to think about their own mortality. We had no reason to expect a gender difference in finitude, and there was none between sons and daughters. As Table 2 shows, there is bivariate evidence that the recent death of the father has a greater impact on the sense of finitude than the death of a mother; the parent's gender, however, does not enter into the multivariate model. Although the age of the parent is not associated with a sense of finitude, it may be that the tendency of fathers to be younger, more independent in daily living makes them appear more similar to the surviving child, than older and less independent mothers, thus threatening the sense of self and increasing a feeling of personal finitude. We are left with the question of whether and how the child's sense of finitude may be associated with the gender of the last parent to die.

In addition to gender as a factor associated with bereavement outcomes, several other characteristics of the parent and child play major roles: the context of the final year of parent's life, the age and socioeconomic status of the child, the child's sense of mastery and feelings of guilt, as well as the quality of the parent-child relationship.

The context of the parent's final year plays a role in the experience of bereavement. The death of parents who had lived in a nursing home was associated with each of the outcomes except somatic response. These deaths are among the most expected because the parent is particularly old and frail. Nursing home deaths may be associated with the most disenfranchised grief [50]. Thus, surviving children may tend to internalize and portray culturally expected reactions to the death: less grief, more control of grief, more acceptance, less sense of personal finitude, and less tie with the dead parent.

Related to the nursing home context is the age of the child (highly correlated with the age of the parent). The younger child may tend to feel the loss is too soon, somewhat off time both in terms of the child's own expectations and the reality of the parent deaths of other members of the child's cohort. Again, death for the older children tends to engender less grief and more acceptance.

Although SES had a strong bivariate association with four of the bereavement outcomes, and it appears in the first step of the regression model, when gender enters the equation for grief, somatic and tie, the SES of the child drops to non-significance. This suggests that SES, which is highly related to gender, seems to be only a weak proxy for gender and has no significant role in explaining grief, somatic and the enduring tie beyond that associated with gender. SES, however, is a strong element in our understanding of acceptance beyond gender, while for finitude gender does not appear to enter into the association between SES and the outcome. These findings in regard to SES suggest some of the complexities in the process of bereavement that can be partially unraveled in multivariate analyses.

Personal mastery is associated with five of the six outcome measures. It is also strongly associated with the child's gender, and for several outcomes it follows a pattern similar to SES above. It appears that only that part of mastery which is associated with gender helps in understanding grief and acceptance. Mastery, on the other hand, plays a role independent of gender in relation to measures of somatic, finitude, and control.

Guilt in not being with or helping the parent enough plays a significant role in explaining control of grief. There may be a pervasive element of negative self appraisal in both guilt and control, such that the surviving child takes a critical stance toward his or her behavior and attitude. In guilt the child is dissatisfied with behavior, in control the child is dissatisfied with pattern of emotional expression. From this perspective, it is understandable why lower personal mastery is associated with greater control. The role of gender in this process is not evident from our data.

The quality of the relationship between the child and parent has a significant impact upon several bereavement outcomes. A more positive relationship is associated with more powerful grief, a stronger tie after the death, and less acceptance of the death. The quality of the parent-child tie, however, does not help us understand the somatic effects of bereavement, the degree of control, or the sense of personal finitude expressed by the child. In subsequent research we are exploring multiple dimensions of the child-parent tie (e.g., positive qualities, negative qualities, and dependency on parent) which in preliminary analyses throw additional light on the interface between the quality of the relationship and the bereavement outcomes.

Although the role of gender has been found to be significant for many bereavement outcomes, we are impressed by the similarities between the findings of our earlier research which focused only on women (daughters of mothers) and this analysis of the four parent-child dyads. The congruity of our findings in our two studies is striking. In both studies we found: grief was explained by younger age and a closer parent-child tie, somatic was explained by less personal mastery, acceptance was explained by older age of the child, finitude by lower personal mastery and more guilt, and the persistence of the tie was explained by the better overall quality of the parent-child relationship. Also children of parents who had lived in a nursing home expressed less grief, more acceptance, and less strong enduring ties. The fact that the findings in this current study in large part replicate our earlier research on DAMOs, suggests that there are strong generic themes in parent loss which tend to be experienced by both sons and daughters of mothers and fathers.

This study has again underlined the importance of examining multiple dimensions of the bereavement process. It has highlighted gender differences in the characteristics of the child, the parent, their relationship as well as in the outcome measures. We have examined how gender plays a major role in the way that adult children respond to their parents' deaths. We suggest that our findings may well have relevance for understanding gendered responses to other family losses.

REFERENCES

1. W. Stroebe and M. Stroebe, *Bereavement and Health*, Cambridge University Press, New York, 1987.
2. M. P. H. D. Cleiren, *Bereavement and Adaptation*, Hemisphere, Washington, D.C., 1993.
3. R. Janoff-Bulman, *Shattered Assumptions*, Free Press, New York, 1992.
4. C. M. Parkes, Bereavement as a Psychosocial Transition: Processes of Adaptation to Change, in *Handbook of Bereavement: Theory, Research and Intervention*, M. S. Stroebe, W. Stroebe, and R. O. Hansson (eds.), Cambridge University Press, New York, pp. 91-101, 1993.
5. C. B. Wortman, R. C. Silver, and R. C. Kessler, The Meaning of Loss and Adjustment to Bereavement, in *Handbook of Bereavement: Theory, Research and Intervention*, M. S. Stroebe, W. Stroebe, and R. O. Hansson (eds.), Cambridge University Press, New York, pp. 349-366, 1993.
6. V. W. Marshall, Age and Awareness of Finitude in Developmental Gerontology, *Omega, Journal of Death and Dying*, 6, pp. 113-129, 1975.

7. T. Attig, The Importance of Conceiving of Grief as an Active Process, *Death Studies*, *15*, pp. 385-393, 1991.
8. D. Klass, P. R. Silverman, and S. Nickman, *Continuing Bonds*, Taylor and Francis, Washington, D.C., 1996.
9. M. Moss, S. Z. Moss, R. Rubinstein, and N. Resch, The Impact of Elderly Mother's Death on Middle Aged Daughters, *International Journal of Aging and Human Development*, *37*, pp. 1-22, 1992.
10. D. A. Lund, Conclusions about Bereavement in Later Life and Implications for Interventions and Future Research, in *Older Bereaved Spouses*, D. A. Lund (ed.), Hemisphere, New York, 1989.
11. M. S. Moss and S. Z. Moss, The Death of a Parent, in *Midlife Loss*, R. A. Kalish (ed.), Sage, Newbury Park, California, pp. 89-114, 1989.
12. H. H. Winsborough, A Demographic Approach to the Life Cycle, in *Life Course: Integrative Theories and Exemplary Populations*, Westview Press, Boulder, Colorado, pp. 65-77, 1980.
13. U.S. Bureau of the Census, *1990 Census of Population and Housing: Summary Population and Housing Characteristics*, U.S. Government Printing Office, Washington, D.C., 1990.
14. J. Bowlby, *Attachment and Loss*, Vol. 1. Attachment, Basic Books, New York, 1969.
15. J. Klapper, S. Z. Moss, M. S. Moss, and R. L. Rubinstein, The Social Context of Grief among Adult Daughters Who have Lost a Parent, *Journal of Aging Studies*, *8*, pp. 29-43, 1994.
16. M. S. Moss and S. Z. Moss, The Impact of Parental Death on Middle-Aged Children, *Omega: Journal of Death and Dying*, *14*, pp. 65-75, 1983-84.
17. I. O. Glick, R. S. Weiss, and C. M. Parkes, *The First Year of Bereavement*, Wiley Interscience, New York, 1974.
18. R. Barnett, L. Beiner, and G. Baruch, *Gender and Stress*, Free Press, New York, 1987.
19. A. R. Hochschild, The Sociology of Feeling and Emotion: Selected Possibilities, in *Another Voice*, M. Millman and R. M. Kanter (eds.), Anchor Books, New York, 1975.
20. N. Chodorov, *The Reproduction of Mothering*, University of California Press, Berkeley, California, 1978.
21. C. Gilligan, *In a Different Voice: Psychological Theory and Women's Development*, Harvard University Press, Cambridge, Massachusetts, 1982.
22. D. Tannen, *You Just Don't Understand: Women and Men in Conversation*, Virago, London, 1990.
23. R. T. Hare-Mustin and J. Marecek, *Making a Difference: Psychology and the Construction of Gender*, Yale University Press, New Haven, Connecticut, 1990.
24. G. Hagestad, The Family: Women and Grandparents as Kinkeepers, in *Our Aging Society*, A. Pifer and L. Bronte (eds.), W. W. Norton, New York, pp. 141-160, 1986.
25. G. Spitze and J. Logan, Sons, Daughters and Intergenerational Support, *Journal of Marriage and Family*, *52*, pp. 420-430, 1990.
26. A. S. Rossi and P. H. Rossi, *Of Human Bonding: Parent-Child Relations across the Life Course*, Aldine de Gruyter, New York, 1990.
27. J. Aldous, E. Klaus, and D. M. Klein, The Understanding Heart: Aging Parents and Their Favorite Child, *Child Development*, *56*, pp. 303-316, 1995.

28. L. Lawton, M. Silverstein, and V. Bengtson, Affection, Social Contact, and Geographic Distance between Adult Children and Their Parents, *Journal of Marriage and the Family, 56*, pp. 57-68, 1994.
29. S. M. Miller and Kirsch, Sex Differences in Cognitive Coping with Stress, in *Gender and Stress*, R. Barnett, L. Biener, and G. Baruch (eds.), Free Press, New York, pp. 278-307, 1987.
30. E. Wethington, J. D. McLeod, and R. C. Kessler, The Importance of Life Events for Explaining Sex Differences in Psychological Distress, in *Gender and Stress*, R. Barnett, L. Biener, and G. K. Baruch (eds.), Free Press, New York, pp. 144-158, 1987.
31. M. Stroebe and W. Stroebe, Who Suffers More? Sex Differences in Health Risks of the Widowed, *Psychological Bulletin, 93*, pp. 297-301, 1983.
32. D. Gallagher-Thompson, A. Futterman, N. Farberow, L. W. Thompson, and J. Peterson, The Impact of Spousal Bereavement on Older Widows and Widowers, in *Handbook of Bereavement: Theory, Research and Intervention*, Cambridge University Press, New York, pp. 227-239, 1993.
33. W. Stroebe and M. S. Stroebe, Determinants of Adjustment to Bereavement in Younger Widows and Widowers, in *Handbook of Bereavement: Theory, Research and Intervention*, M. S. Stroebe, W. Stroebe, and R. O. Hansson (eds.), Cambridge University Press, New York, pp. 208-226, 1993.
34. D. A. Lund, M. S. Caserta, and M. F. Dimond, The Course of Spousal Bereavement in Later Life, in *Handbook of Bereavement: Theory, Research and Intervention*, M. S. Stroebe, W. Stroebe, and R. O. Hansson (eds.), Cambridge University Press, New York, pp. 240-254, 1993.
35. D. Umberson, C. B. Wortman, and R. C. Kessler, Widowhood and Depression: Explaining Long-Term Gender Differences in Vulnerability, *Journal of Health and Human Behavior, 33*, pp. 10-24, 1992.
36. N. W. Arbuckle and B. de Vries, The Long Term Effects of Later Life Spousal and Parental Bereavement on Personal Functioning, *The Gerontologist, 35*, pp. 637-647, 1995.
37. J. Littlewood, *Aspects of Grief: Bereavement in Adult Life*, Tavistock, New York, 1992.
38. P. R. Silverman and J. W. Worden, Children's Reactions to the Death of a Parent, in *Handbook of Bereavement: Theory, Research and Intervention*, M. Stroebe, W. Stroebe, and R. O. Hansson (eds.), Cambridge University Press, New York, pp. 300-316, 1993.
39. D. Umberson, *The Impact of Death of a Parent on Adult Children's Psychological Well Being: A Prospective Study*, paper presented at the annual scientific meeting of the Gerontological Society of America, Boston, 1990.
40. A. E. Scharlach, Factors Associated with Filial Grief following the Death of an Elderly Parent, *American Journal of Orthopsychiatry, 61*, pp. 307-312, 1991.
41. P. Popek and A. E. Scharlach, Adult Daughters' Relationship with Their Mothers and Reactions to Their Mothers' Deaths, *Journal of Women and Aging, 3*, pp. 79-96, 1991.
42. C. M. Parkes and R. S. Weiss, *Recovery from Bereavement*, Basic Books, New York, 1983.

43. M. P. Lawton, M. Moss, and A. Glicksman, The Quality of the Last Year of Life of Older Persons, *Milbank Quarterly, 68*, pp. 1-28, 1991.
44. L. Pearlin and C. Schooler, The Structure of Coping, *Journal of Health and Social Behavior, 19*, pp. 2-21, 1978.
45. N. Bradburn, *The Structure of Psychological Well-Being*, Aldine, Chicago, 1969.
46. T. R. Faschingbauer, S. Zisook, and R. A. De Vaul, The Texas Revised Inventory of Grief, in *Biopsychosocial Aspects of Bereavement*, S. Zisook (ed.), American Psychiatric Press, Washington, D.C., pp. 111-124, 1987.
47. V. W. Marshall, *Last Chapters: A Sociology of Aging and Dying*, Brooks/Cole, Monterey, California, 1980.
48. A. Bower, *Gender, Acceptance of Parent Death and Expressivity*, presented at annual meeting of Gerontological Society of America, Los Angeles, 1995.
49. S. Z. Moss and R. L. Rubinstein, *Middle-Aged Son's Reactions to Father's Death*, presented at the annual meeting of the Gerontological Society of America, Los Angeles, California, 1995.
50. M. S. Moss and S. Z. Moss, Death and Bereavement, in *Handbook of Aging and the Family*, R. Blieszner and V. H. Bedford (eds.), Greenwood Press, Westport, Connecticut, pp. 422-439, 1995.

THE ADULT CHILD'S ACCEPTANCE OF PARENT DEATH*

ANNE R. BOWER, PH.D.
Polisher Research Institute,
Philadelphia Geriatric Center, Pennsylvania

ABSTRACT

In the grief and bereavement literature, the discussion of acceptance often regards it as an end-point of the process and utilizes a definition that is linked to duration and intensity of grief. The study of parent death is no exception. Adult children are rarely asked whether or why they have or have not accepted the death of an elderly parent, or even what acceptance means to them. The extent to which such studies accurately report on the experience of parent death acceptance is questionable. Using ethnographic and linguistic techniques, this study approaches acceptance through a qualitative examination of adult children's verbatim responses to direct inquiries about their acceptance of an elderly parent's death. Findings indicate that while the majority of adult children readily assert acceptance of their parent's death, these assertions are contingent upon important beliefs and values relating to the death, the power of feelings, and the strength of memory. Further, and most important, acceptance appears to be a phenomenon adult children feel compelled to explain.

ACCEPTANCE IN THE BEREAVEMENT LITERATURE

The importance of acceptance in current conceptualizations of the course of grief is indisputable. The bereavement literature discusses acceptance in a variety of ways, treating it as a necessary and important part of grief. Yet, perhaps the most

---

*This research was funded by National Institute on Aging Grant R01-AG10875: Children's Perspective on Death of an Elderly Parent, Robert L. Rubinstein, P.I.

© 1997, Baywood Publishing Co., Inc.

striking feature of the literature's treatment of acceptance is that the researcher's voice predominates. Apart from the occasional case note, single-sentence verbatim quote, or single word "descriptors" to give the "flavor" of respondents' comments, the clearest voice we hear in the literature is that of the researcher or clinician. The voices of the bereaved speaking about their own acceptance of a loved one's death are markedly absent.

A review of the literature suggests that the role assigned to acceptance in bereavement theory is more likely to reflect the researchers' theoretical views and personal intuitions about what acceptance *is* or *ought to be* rather than reflecting an inquiry into acceptance or their subjects' perceptions of acceptance. For example, acceptance is widely discussed as a *desirable outcome* to grief and, as such, is typically situated in the broad context of grief's course, often as the last in a sequence of grief-related "tasks" or "work" [1-14]. Acceptance is linked explicitly to other experiential states attributed to grieving, such as *recognition* [3], *recovery* [15], *resignation* [16], or used interchangeably with *resolution* [17], but is rarely accompanied by discussion about the reasons for such conceptual alignments. Acceptance is differentiated according to type, again with little explication, *emotional* and *cognitive* acceptance [2, 8, 18] or *conscious* and *unconscious* acceptance [8]. Other research isolates acceptance in respondents' agreement or disagreement with statements about the *timeliness* or *fairness* of the parent's death [9, 18] or about *satisfying* and *unsatisfying* aspects of the parent/child tie [10, 16]. Given the centrality of bereaved people to our research, and given the important role of acceptance in our understanding of bereavement, acceptance deserves an examination that is more closely attentive to the voices of the bereaved rather than to the researcher's voice.

Consequently, the purpose of this discussion is to examine acceptance of an elderly, widowed parent's death from adult children's point of view and in their own words. By asking recently bereaved sons or daughters what they have to say about their own experience of acceptance, and then listening closely to both what they say and how they say it, I contend that we can better understand what constitutes acceptance and how it is experienced. In the discussion to follow, we will approach acceptance by identifying four key features of the discourse. One of these is that acceptance is a heavily explained phenomenon. The content of participants' explanation for their acceptance and non-acceptance will be explored. We will then consider how the overall structure and specific language of acceptance talk relates explanatory content to participants' affirmations and denials of acceptance. Finally, we will consider the explaining nature of acceptance talk as a structural characteristic of the experience rather than as an artifact of the interview context.

The present study takes its inspiration from recent research in cultural anthropology which argues that the experience of emotion, such as grief, is culturally constructed [19-22] and analytically accessible through discourse [23, 24]. This perspective contends that grief is conveyed through verbal modalities, such as oratory, wailing, poetry or ordinary talk, and cannot be separated from their verbal expression. Further, verbal expression cannot be separated from the context of its occurrence [25, 26]. Following this perspective, this discussion will regard acceptance of parent death as one aspect of the "lived experience" of grief [27]. As such, the nature of the experience of acceptance should be accessible through examination of talk about it. Acceptance talk will be examined through ethnographic analysis of its content and application of sociolinguistic analytic techniques to its specific language and structure. The result will be a realistic close-up picture of acceptance that assists in further understanding and defining this important aspect of grief.

THE DATA

The Sample

The sample of fifty respondents used in this analysis is drawn from a larger ongoing study of 240 participants aimed at understanding the adult child's perspective on the death of an elderly parent. The specific aim of the parent death study is to understand the death as both a loss and as a life course transition for the adult child, specifically the affect of parent death on the adult child's perceptions of self, personal continuity, and well-being. The effect of care giving circumstances on children's understanding of the meaning of their parents' death is also an important focus of the study, as is the role of gender in affecting perspective on parent death.

An in-depth, semi-structured ethnographic interview was conducted with each of the 240 participants. Interviews ranged between two to four hours in length, and were audiotape-recorded with the respondents' permission. The interviews were conducted six to eight months after parent's death; long enough after the death for the respondent to have begun to make sense of the experience, yet close enough to it to constitute a recent bereavement. The deceased parent was a widowed mother or father, sixty-five years or older.

In this study of acceptance, a total of fifty respondents is represented: twenty-seven daughters and twenty-three sons. Three age categories are represented: forty to forty-nine years ($n = 18$); fifty to fifty-nine years ($n = 19$) and sixty to sixty-five years ($n = 13$), and three caregiving categories: heavy caregiving ($n = 14$); nursing home ($n = 18$) and light or no caregiving ($n = 18$). While the sex, age, and caregiving status of the respondent will not figure in this analysis, the interaction of these variables with adult sons' and daughters' reaction is addressed in Moss et al.'s article, "The Role of Gender in Middle-Age Children's Responses to Parent Death," in this volume.

Description of the Data

The data for this discussion are participants' tape-recorded responses to the open-ended question about acceptance:

> Some [sons/daughters] say they have accepted their [mother's/father's] death and others say they have not fully accepted the death. How was it for you?

The introduction of this topic is deeply embedded in the discussion of the respondent's emotional reaction to his or her parent's death, which initiates and occupies the first hour or more of the interview. The acceptance question is situated in a sequence of topics that moves from the opening request for the respondent to tell the story of the parent's death to the daughter's or son's initial reaction to the death, the importance or meaning of being with the parent at the moment of death, subsequent reactions to the death; prior thoughts about the parent's death and concerns about what reaction she or he might have to the death, the need for and value of controlling emotion surrounding the death, *the daughter's or son's acceptance of the death* and finally to a comparison of parent's death to other significant deaths over the years.

Participants' responses to this question were transcribed verbatim, in full. This included all of the respondent's talk in response to the question and on any additional topics stimulated by the acceptance talk. Interviewer comments and reactions were also transcribed verbatim, in full. Non-verbal components of the response, such as tears, laughter, coughs, sighs, or pauses, were also noted in the transcription as potentially important sources of information about the respondent's understanding of or reaction to the issue or acceptance. Kinesic behavior can also be laden with meaning in some situations. Consequently, behavior such as tapping the edge of a spoon on the side of a cup for emphasis as one son did, or jumping up from the table in mid-statement to adjust the air-conditioning level as another daughter did, were also noted in the transcriptions. The response to the acceptance question was regarded as completed when the respondent fell silent or otherwise indicated by word or other conversational behavior that her or his turn at talk on this topic had concluded. The interviewer then asked the next question.

The following examples illustrate the variety of response to the acceptance question, and the type of verbatim transcript used in this study. In each case, the question is asked as indicated above. The interviewer's comments are in parentheses. At the close of each quotation, the speaker's age is indicated, followed by an abbreviation of the parent/child dyad: DA/MO refers to daughter/mother, SO/FA to son/father, DA/FA refers to daughter/father, and SO/MO to son/mother.

> Accepted it, yes. Because I know it was God's will. Had it not been His will, she would be here now. She may be a vegetable. I would probably be more

tired now than when I was running back and forth to the hospital. But it was God's will that she should leave us. So, I have accepted it. Yes, I miss her, but that's to be expected. But, I accept God's will. (65, DA/MO)

I accepted—[pauses, tapping spoon against side of coffee mug]—my father's death because I know everybody has to die, OK? And as I—and I said it previously, I could accept it a lot easier considering his age, and the fact that he was here with us. He wasn't alone, you know what I mean? And you just—you just can't ignore the eventuality. (45, SO/FA)

Yeah. Yeah. Yeah. Yeah. You know—I mean—I'm not looking forward to him walking through that door! No. But, I have. I have because, like I said, it's a natural thing, OK? And this is it. (45, SO/FA)

Well-it-uh—sure, I accepted it because I know he's dead. Hehhehehheh, OK? Uhm—. (Sure.) I—like I said, I still dream of him. And most of [my] dreams are of him comin' back, OK? And-uh-like me, I'm like: "No! Don't come back!" Yeah, I did accept it, because he isn't here, and I-I know he can't be here, but I can talk to him all the time. (43, DA/FA)

Oh, I'm over the death, if that's what you mean. There's no cost in going back over it, or anything like that. I'm over it. Death happens. It happened. (63, SO/MO)

I've accepted it. [Tearful, blowing nose] When I say that I accept it, I know that he is gone, but not gone, because [sobs] he'll always be [voice breaks] in my heart. (Mhhhmmm.) But I know he's at peace. And he's not suffering anymore. And that makes me feel better because I loved him too much to see him suffer. I didn't want him to be here suffering, you know. [Sobs, takes a deep breath, blows nose.] (61, DA/FA)

Oh, I've accepted it. Absolutely. (58, SO/MO)

These examples communicate something of the complex and ambiguous content and feeling in the response to the acceptance question. Let us turn now to a discussion of the content, structure, and language of acceptance.

KEY FEATURES OF ACCEPTANCE DISCOURSE

Four striking characteristics define respondents' discussion of acceptance. First, response to the acceptance query was swift; second, the proportion of affirmative responses was high; third, acceptance was not easily described by respondents; but, fourth, acceptance was readily and extensively explained.

Swiftness of the Response

Respondents did not hesitate in their reply to the acceptance question. Whether accepting or not, they answered swiftly and surely, often beginning to speak while the interviewer was still asking the question, effectively interrupting the interviewer. The meaning of respondents' ready answer to the acceptance question lends itself to speculation, some of which will be addressed in the concluding discussion. Suffice it here to say that such behavior at least suggests that respondents felt this to be an aspect of their experience of the death that they could comment on readily.

The Affirmative Response

Forty-five of the fifty respondents said: Yes, I have accepted my parent's death. Five respondents said: No, I have not. The near unanimity of the reaction suggests that the notion of acceptance taps a fundamental experience relevant to respondents.

An Experience Difficult to Describe

Interestingly, despite the alacrity of their affirmative response, respondents felt that "acceptance" was a term they were unlikely to have used themselves in thinking about their parent's death or in talking about it with others. It was not a term foremost in their minds as they talked about their bereavement. Only a few respondents spontaneously introduced acceptance into the discussion before the interviewer did. Respondents rarely returned to the issue of acceptance at later points in the interview, and acceptance was rarely developed as a separate theme in the overall discourse. Rather, once they had addressed, explored and talked about acceptance, respondents tended to leave the topic. In this regard, acceptance is unlike other topics to which respondents returned again and again throughout the interview in one guise or another, for example, the physical sensations of grief or particular character traits of the deceased parent, or the effects of parent death on perceptions of personal finitude.

Explaining Acceptance

Despite the apparent unfamiliarity of the term, once the topic was introduced, respondents had a considerable amount to say about it. Very few affirmed or denied acceptance without offering their further thoughts, feelings, and reactions. Some participants gave lengthy answers to the question, others were quite brief. However, the son who responded: "Oh, I've accepted it. Absolutely" without further discussion was atypical.

While acceptance discourse appears to be widely varied in content, an underlying structure is discernible. Acceptance talk displays a distinctive, three-part organization, irrespective of content: *claim + connecting word + statements*. A review of the three parts offers a clearer view of how each component operates to construct an explanation. First, as we have seen, the respondent asserts his or her acceptance of the death in a declarative sentence in direct response to the acceptance query. Whether its content is affirmative, negative, ambiguous, or some kinesic behavior such as a head-nod is structurally irrelevant. All respondents initiate their response with such a claim. Moving out of sequence for a moment, the next component of the structure is the verbal statement(s) respondents offer to instantiate, validate, or support their claim. The single sentence or sentence clusters that follow the claim constitute the material for the analysis of themes. The final component of the structure is a single word which links, relates or connects the claim to the following statements. In these data, *because*, and *but* appear more frequently, although others also appear, such as *only* and *just*. In some cases, no connective appears to link claims to following statements.

However individualized respondents' acceptance talk appears to be on the surface, it nevertheless demonstrates the same underlying structure. Interestingly, this structure is similar to other types of discourse units identified in the symbolic interactionist literature, notably accounts [28-31], disclaimers [32, 33] or vernacular argument [34]. Like acceptance talk, these discourse units function to provide explanations, justifications, accounts of, and arguments for positions articulated in the social exchange. Identifying this structure in acceptance talk permits us to see and affirm its explanatory nature.

EXPLAINING ACCEPTANCE: THEMES

While respondents may have difficulty describing their experience of acceptance, they can readily explain it. If acceptance is an experiential state that seemingly must be explained, what explanations do respondents then offer for it? In this section, we will identify and examine the major themes that are articulated in the talk that follows respondents' acceptance claims. Exploration of the thematic content of respondents' supporting statements offers not only additional insight into their experience of acceptance but also insight into how respondents define and think about their acceptance.

In all, ten different themes emerged from the acceptance discourse of the fifty participants. These themes are immediately differentiated by their co-occurrence with either affirmative or negative claims of acceptance. The majority (45/50) of respondents claim that they have accepted their parent's death. Six salient themes emerge as support for these affirmative claims. The remainder (5/50) claim that they have not accepted their parent's death. Three different themes emerge in this latter discourse. An additional theme is articulated by both accepting and non-accepting respondents. Each theme is identified by a reference title that captures its content. In order of frequency of mention, the six themes that emerge in accepting respondents' discourse are as follows:

1. Death as a fact
2. Death as endpoint
3. Strong feelings
4. Death as God's will
5. Death as part of the natural order
6. Parent as memory

Since the majority of respondents do claim that they accept their parent's death, these represent the core themes in respondents' discussion of acceptance. In contrast, fewer themes emerge in the discourse of the respondents who maintain that they have not accepted their parent's death. Again, in order of frequency of mention, the non-acceptance themes include:

7. Maintaining interaction
8. An unacceptable death
9. Unresolved problems

One theme was defined by the varying ways in which it co-occurred with the acceptance claim.

10. The intimacy of caregiving

Methods for Analyzing Themes

Three analytic approaches were used to identify, analyze, and explicate the themes that appear in acceptance talk. First, using a sociolinguistic technique for arranging and displaying discourse structure, acceptance responses were regarded as simply a sequence of clauses, irrespective of meaning [35]. Each clause was assigned to a separate line. Second, each line or cluster of lines were analyzed for topic, summarized according to topic, and counted as one instance of mention. Lines with similar topics were grouped together. Recurrent topics were grouped together and summarized to describe their shared elements of content. Recurring topics were then identified as themes in the acceptance discourse, i.e., as principal subjects in the supporting statements [36, 37]. The frequency of particular themes and respondents' direct statements about their importance served as indications of their salience in the discussion of acceptance. The acceptance discourse of each respondent was subjected to the sociolinguistic and thematic analyses outlined above.

Third, special attention was paid to respondents' language. The words used to link claims of acceptance to explanatory statements were of particular interest because they provided further insight into how explanations are related to claims. Two connectives appeared most frequently in the acceptance discourse: *because* and *but*. Given the variety of words a speaker might use in connecting his or her acceptance claim to explanatory statements, the predominance of these two suggests that they communicate widely shared and important elements of the acceptance experience [38, 39]. The meaning of these linking words was analyzed using the discourse analytic technique of semantic expansion [40, 41] which identifies and explicates a target word's semantic meaning and grammatical properties in the specific context of its occurrence.

The Acceptance Themes

Respondents who say they have accepted their parent's death support these claims with statements about the nature of death or the power of personal feeling and memory. The six acceptance themes are recalled below along with their realization in respondents' discourse.

Death as a Fact

In statements grouped under this heading, respondents articulate a cognitive understanding and recognition of the physical fact of death, often characterizing it as "a reality," "a fact," or "inevitable."

> Yeah, I did accept it because he isn't here, and I know he can't be here. (43, DA/FA)

> Well, I'm very practical. You have to accept it. It's—it's a fact . . . a physical fact. (55, DA/MO)

> Uhm-naturally I've-I've accepted it, you know what I mean? Because she's dead. (65, SO/MO)

> Yeah, yeah, yeah. You know-uh-I mean I'm not looking forward to him walking through that door. (45, SO/FA)

Death's factuality, its immutability, its irreversibility becomes the focus, the issue to which the respondent relates. The individual parent's death is subsumed into the factuality of the experience. The notion of a lack of "choice" is frequently articulated in this context. The unretractable nature of death forces them into acceptance.

> You know that you don't have no choice but to accept it. (65, DA/MO)

> Yeah, I don't think you have a choice, do you? It's a done deal. They don't come back. You can't call up the church and say "Hey! Mom's not supposed to die this week! Send her back! (52, DA/MO)

Death as Endpoint

In statements that articulate this theme, the elder's death represents the endpoint to some trajectory, such as a long life, a long illness, or a long relationship.

> OK, and as I said, I could accept it a lot easier considering his age. (68, SO/FA)

One daughter linked her acceptance of her ninety-three-year-old father's death to his longevity:

> Oh, yes. I am sure I have [accepted it]. Fortunately, he was as old as he was. Well, in our family, anything over 90 is acceptable. Before that, it's before their time. (64, DA/FA)

For one son, acceptance of his elderly mother's death in a nursing home was linked, by implication, to her age but explicitly situated in the context of his own age, which was sixty-three years:

> I accept it, yeah . . . [At my age] if our parents are still alive, it's only a matter of time before they are going to pass away. And I guess when it happened to me, it was easier to accept. (63, SO/MO)

Death also figures as the endpoint to the trajectory of the parent's steadily declining physical condition, or it ends a period in the parent's life in which his or her reduced psychosocial circumstances made the quality of life untenable. For most respondents in these circumstances, a parent's death is not an unwelcome endpoint, however many still bolster this view with a reference to their parent's earlier, stated wish not to live past a certain age or in a deteriorating physical condition. Some project backwards, arguing that death was the outcome the *parent* would have wished for in the face of such circumstances.

> I mean, probably part of [my accepting] is because I know that my mother wouldn't have—wouldn't have wanted to live the way that she was living in the last year of her life. (50, DA/MO)

> Yes, I have accepted it. There was actually-uh-nothing for her to live for. She indeed had said there was nothing for her to do. (44, SO/MO)

While most respondents articulate this theme from the parent's perspective, i.e., the trajectory ended the parent's long life or unhappy circumstances, the comments of others shift the vantage point. It is not death as endpoint to the parent's life that becomes the focus, but rather, death as endpoint to the trajectory of the parent/child relationship. Implicit in this view is the notion of a "fair" time period during which the child can legitimately "have" a parent with him or her, but after which there can be no claim to sadness since the time together was long.

> Well, I have accepted it for the simple reason that I had my mother a long time. I had her for—well, since I was a baby, and—. Actually, I have had her for 58 years, from the day I was born up until the day she died. And I didn't turn 59 until last July. So, I had her a long time. (59, DA/MO)

This daughter goes on to say that she relinquished her mother without bitterness, grateful for the time they had together. Another daughter explicitly characterized this trajectory as a "loan" from God. God called in the loan, and mother died.

> I've given [her] up. (Given up?) Given her up to God. Because, if you look at it, she was only loaned to us for a while. Then, God reclaims His own. (65, DA/MO)

For a few respondents, the parent's death represented a receipt for a final payment in an unseen, divine, moral transaction that was understood by the child only in retrospect. For example, in discussing his acceptance of his father's death, one son observed that his father regarded his terminal cancer as punishment for the sins of his younger days. His father often spoke of "paying his debts" and his illness in the same breath, but it was not until after his father died that this son understood what his father had meant:

> Because Pop had said: I'm being punished for the things that I have done, you know, for the way that I was. But, the thing is, I'm still here, you know, so I must have more to pay. When that's up, I'll be gone, you know.
> And that's what happened. And at the time, I really never thought about that. But after he died, I said: Wow! I guess Pop paid all his debts!
> You know, because that's one of the things he said. He said: I guess all the debts that I have, once they're paid, I'll be gone. (That's a very interesting point of view.) Yeah. And I said: I can go along with that. (45, SO/FA)

Strong Feelings

Specific, strong, personal reactions to the parent's death occupy the supporting statements of some respondents, typically feelings of anger, sadness, or longing. In this thematic category, the confluence of the cognitive and emotional parameters of acceptance are articulated most clearly. Revelations of strong emotions are mentioned in the same breath with claims of accepting the elder's death, and often with statements that reflect the death as fact theme. However, the nature of the relationship between acceptance and explanation is realized in two different ways in this thematic category. For some respondents, the emotional parameter is subordinated to the rational acknowledgment of the death. For example, one daughter explained her acceptance of her father's death by placing it in the context of her anger at his decision to hasten his own death by declining medical treatment:

> I've accepted it, because that's the way it is. It's just sad. I'm not over him leaving. And I'm——. I think I'm kind of angry at him for signing that paper [to decline medical treatment], because he'd still be here. But I can't yell at him now. (42, DA/FA)

Confounding acceptance with equanimity, another daughter found it difficult to respond to the question about acceptance:

> It-I still get angry about it. Is that not accepting it? I mean, it's a reality, you know. (50, DA/MO)

For these respondents, the claim of acceptance is *situated* in the emotional experience described in the explanatory statements. Feelings of anger, sadness, or longing define an emotional context in which the death is oriented to as a physical reality, and accepted.

For other respondents, however, strong feelings appear to exist *in opposition* to their claims of acceptance. The key to this reading lies in the meaning of the linking word *but* which connects the acceptance claim to the supporting statements that follow it.

> I have, yeah, *but* it was—sad. You know, it——. You just miss her so much. I-I-knew that it would be the best thing, *but* I just miss her. And I sure thought *I would* miss her a lot! (55, DA/MO)

> I have accepted it, *but* I still think of him and I still miss him, especially at special moments. (60, SO/FA)

> I don't think you have a choice. You accept it, *but*—uhm—I don't think you can let go that way. That dependency—need—is still always there, no matter what. (43, DA/FA)

More will be said about *but* in the next section. Suffice it here to say that, in acceptance claims explained with *but*-statements, the strong emotional states of anger, sadness or longing are brought into direct opposition with the claim of acceptance, each weighted equally. *But*-statements as explanations argue for the equivalence of acceptance and strong feelings. For these respondents, anger, sadness, and longing are not absorbed into the equanimity of acceptance as they appear to be for respondents who link their acceptance to the physical (or spiritual) factuality of death. Rather, strong feelings exist in full, equally weighted counterpoint to equally strong feelings of acceptance. As such, these statements reveal an experience of acceptance that positions cognitive and emotional reactions as opposing equivalents.

It is tempting to regard both the "situated" and the "contrastive" statements of strong feelings as qualified statements of acceptance. Yet, in my view, this is not an accurate reading of respondents' comments. "Qualified" suggests an element of limitation or restriction placed upon the acceptance by the strong feelings that are articulated. Neither "situated" nor "contrastive" statements in these data appear to offer such restrictions. Rather, the language of such statements suggests that strong feelings are not experienced as limitations upon acceptance, but rather as a context in which the acceptance occurs or as an independent state in direct opposition to acceptance.

Death as God's Will

Respondents regard the death as God's will for their parent. They acknowledge that the gravity of the parent's medical condition made death a certain outcome, but they speak of these conditions as having developed according to God's plan. The effects of very advanced years, terminal illness, decline and death itself, are interpreted as manifesting God's will. Some respondents employ "mystery words" [42] to refer demurely to this guiding power, while others are explicit in their attribution:

> Oh, I've accepted her death. She was in dire extremities for a long time. It's a miracle she lived that long. (55, DA/MO)

> And I think [I also accept it]. I think it was God's time. He wanted her. God wanted her, and I know she's at peace now. (57, DA/MO)

> I accepted it. I accepted it because I knew it was God's will. (46, DA/FA)

> But it was God's will that she should leave us. So I have accepted it. (65, DA/MO)

Death as Part of the Natural Order

Death is accepted on the grounds that it is part of life and will be experienced by all living beings. As such, death can be met with equanimity and accepted.

> Yes, I have accepted it, because dying is part of living, you know. I mean, it's what happens. (44, SO/MO)

> I accepted my father's death because I know everybody has to die . . . You just can't ignore the eventuality. (65, SO/FA)

> Oh, fully accepted it. Absolutely. It's part of life. (59, SO/MO)

> Yeah, I have, because, like I said, it's the natural thing, OK? And this is—this is it. (45, SO/FA)

Both child and parent come to be seen as elements in the natural order and follow a progression through a natural life cycle: the old die, the young survive and accept the death, with the knowledge that they, too, will die.

The Natural Order theme is related in subtle, yet important, ways to other themes that emerge in the acceptance discourse, specifically Death as Fact, Death as Endpoint, and Death as God's Will. For example, Natural Order is similar to the Death as Fact theme in that they both invoke a schema of natural, physical fact within which the adult child's acceptance and the parent's death are interpreted. Yet, the two themes differ in the identity death assumes in each. In explanations that involve the factuality of death, death is positioned as an isolated occurrence. The respondent neither refers to nor implies what came before the death (unlike the Endpoint theme), or what may come after. The Natural Order theme differs from Death as Fact in this regard since such Natural Order explanations anchor death in a natural, recurring cycle in which events (implicitly or explicitly) are positioned as variously preceding the death and proceeding from the death.

Natural Order is differentiated from Death as Endpoint by its scope. Natural Order is global or inclusive of all experience, while Endpoint focuses on the final point in some lengthy personal trajectory, whether longevity, illness, or moral obligations.

Finally, unlike the Death as God's Will theme, which interprets the parent's death as a divine expression, statements that articulate Natural Order appear to construe death as an experience without spiritual or supernatural associations. In this regard, it is reminiscent of the philosophical school of naturalism [43].

Parent as Memory

The parent's living personality and identity can be transformed into a memory that the son or daughter can then hold close in mind or heart. Acceptance is linked to this transformation, which takes a variety of shapes. For example, it may involve forging a collective memory or interpretation of the deceased parent through talk with siblings:

> My brothers and sisters, we just reminisce about all the nice times we had together. And that's what makes me accept. (57, DA/MO)

The entirety of the parent's character and personality may be transformed into memory through the individual's solitary remembering. As one son says about his mother:

> Oh yeah, yeah. I have accepted [it]. My mother is a—it's a memory. I sometimes get up and look at her pictures, and so forth, and say: I don't want to forget. I don't want to forget who she was and what she was to me. (64, SO/MO)

For others, the transformation is accomplished by "seeing" with mother's or father's eye. For example, this son's acceptance of his father's death is linked to his ability to appreciate the youngsters of the family with his father's eye:

> Yes, no question about [accepting it]. Sometimes I think about certain things, that if he were here to—. More of the appreciative things. Especially with the grandchildren because he was really crazy about the little ones. (65, SO/FA)

For still others, the deceased parent may simply be transferred from his or her space in the living world to a continued life in the respondent's memory or heart.

> Uhm-uh-naturally I've accepted it, you know what I mean, because she's dead. But-uh-to me, she lives in my—on in my memory. (65, SO/MO)

> When I say I accept, I know he is gone, but not gone because [sobs] he'll always be [sobs] in my heart. (61, DA/FA)

Note that the language of these "living on" statements strongly resembles that of the Strong Feelings statements. Here again, *but* is the key word in communicating the complex experience of acceptance that both acknowledges the factuality of death while defining an equal and opposite experience. In Strong Feelings statements, *but* ushered in the assertion of a grieving inner state that exists in contrast to acceptance. Similarly, in the "living on" statements in this thematic category, *but* introduces powerful, individual counter-challenges to Death's omniscient factuality: ". . . she's dead, but to me, she lives on in . . .": ". . . I know he is gone, but not gone . . .".

The Non-Acceptance Themes

Five (of 50) adult children represented in this study said they have not accepted their parent's death and offered supporting statements that articulated concrete, literal interpretations of their own and others' behaviors.

Non-acceptance themes differ dramatically from acceptance themes. While acceptance themes are evanescent, non-acceptance themes are concrete. Where

82 / BOWER

accepting respondents' supporting statements invoke beliefs about the nature of death and the power of emotion or memory, non-accepting respondents' statements articulate observations of behavior. The three non-acceptance themes differ in content, but they share roots in the observation of behavior, rather than beliefs about philosophical concepts.

Maintaining Interaction

Death is not an endpoint for respondents who articulated this theme. Interaction with the deceased parent is sought or carried out in several contexts, both waking and sleeping. For example, in waking hours, interaction is maintained through thoughts about the parent's welfare, medication, or medical treatment schedule, scheduling time to give care to or run errands for the parent, picking up the telephone to place a call to the parent, only to recall with a jolt that such care giving is no longer required. In sleeping contexts, respondents dream about their deceased parent, hold dream-time conversations, or see an image of their parent's face or figure in the room as they wake. Items in their parents' rooms have not been changed, the home or room has not been "cleaned out," clothing has not been given away, and personal artifacts, such as a shaving kit, a favorite pair of old shoes, a walker, an old fox collar, a stack of knitting magazines, unused medications, remain in place. Respondents regard maintaining interaction in these ways as indicative of non-acceptance, and non-accepting respondents consistently interpreted their own behavior in this light.

> I don't think I've really accepted it, when I think realistically, because I'm still—still in and out of his house. I-I can still see-uhm-maybe a book over there that he read, because basically, everything is still the same way. (43, DA/FA)

> I-I-like I said, I still dream of him. And most of my dreams are of him coming back, OK. And I-I know he can't be here-uh-uh-but I can talk to him all the time. (Do you talk with him?) Oh yeah, every night. See, Ralph works from 12 to 8. And I'm here by myself. And-uh-I say: Dad! Don't forget! Don't le[t] no one get me! And I'll lay in bed and I'll say: Stand at my bed! (Have you seen him again?) No. No. With my eyes open? No. Nope. (But just in your dreams?) In my dreams, all the time. (43, DA/FA)

A few respondents, such as the daughter quoted immediately above, were comforted by their efforts to maintain interaction with their parent, but most were discomfited by what they regard as their inability to "let go." Another daughter's comment (quoted in full in the discussion of intimacy and caregiving to follow) bears repeating in this context because it is a question non-accepting respondents ask themselves. In describing her "continued" but now unnecessary review of her daily caregiving responsibilities for her deceased father, she asks: "What am I doing? Am I cracking up, you know? Am I really losing it?"

An Unacceptable Death

A second theme in non-accepting respondents' supporting statements is that the cause or the manner of the parent's death was unacceptable to them. They did not believe their parent's death was a necessary result of the terminal condition the medical authorities claim that it was, or even that their parent was properly diagnosed or treated. They did not accept the manner in which they believe their parent died, for example, unattended or disregarded by the medical staff charged with his or her care, alone, in pain, thirsty, and so on.

> Well, as I said, I do not believe my father had to die. I think that his illness was not treated aggressively by the Northtown Hospital, nor was what he had diagnosed properly by the attending physician at the Northtown Home. So that's my thoughts and feelings. I do not believe that he had to die. (44, SO/FA)

> [What I can't accept is not the death,] it's the thing leading up to the death or the thing coming after the death. The death is not the—the main factor to me. It's like——. Some people say: You must die with dignity. I didn't feel as though pulling the plug on my father was [letting him] die with dignity. I looked at it like [this]: he was black, he was poor, he was on medicare. They did not want to give him the proper care. It wasn't "dignity." (46, DA/FA)

> I didn't accept the way he went [i.e., alone, in pain]. Even though I can't change the way he went. I wouldn't wish that on anyone, the way he went. I don't think he was deserving of such a death. (45, SO/FA)

While these respondents may briefly acknowledge the fact of their parent's death, such an acknowledgment fades before their preoccupation with the circumstances leading up to the death. Their responses are the longest in the sample, and are composed of lengthy, detailed reviews of events, self-examination and second-guessing, challenges to decisions that were made, and repeated descriptions of "better" decisions, which, if they had been made, would have resulted in their parent's recovery. Note that the source of the obstacles to acceptance is externally located, while in the previous theme, the source of the obstacles is located within the respondent.

Unresolved Problems

In the third non-accepting theme, the source of the obstacle to acceptance lies within the family, experienced as friction between siblings regarding settlement of parent's estate or a significant illness in another family member. While this theme appears infrequently in talk about acceptance, it is strongly articulated where it does appear. Such circumstances dominate the respondent's attention and complicate his or her experience of acceptance. Two examples illustrate the complex situations that characterize this theme.

One daughter said that she had not accepted her mother's death and supported that claim with references to an angry and estranged relationship with her brother. She revealed a gummy situation in which her own acceptance of her mother's death was dependent upon her perceptions of her mother's peaceful rest, which in turn was dependent upon the resolution of mother's financial difficulties, which could only be realized through a reconciliation with her brother. Her two aunts, her mother's sisters, introduced yet another level of complexity as they tried to convince her that this tangled impasse represented her mother's post-mortem efforts to bring her two children into alignment with each other:

> If I could resolve her estate, then I-I think I could rest knowing she's at peace. But as long as her estate [is unsettled], and there is any disagreement between my brother and I, she'll never be fully at rest. (So, it's both the estate and what goes on between you and your brother?) Yeah. I've tried, but he doesn't want to respond.
>
> [Both my aunts] believe that it's my mother holding up the will. They believe—they try talking me into this—they say: Your mother's holding up the will until youse two get together. It's your mother holding up the will until you two talk to each other again. (What do you think?) I can't believe it. It's him! I've tried, but he doesn't want to respond. And I said to my aunt: How much longer can I keep pushing him? It's his turn to come back to me now. I've done my half. If he can't accept [the death], I-I-I can't help him. (40, DA/MO)

A second example reflects a less complicated, but no less powerful, situation in which the respondent articulated this theme. This daughter's very elderly mother died in a nursing home after several years of Alzheimer's Disease. Shortly before her mother's death, her husband was diagnosed as having advanced prostate cancer. At the time of the interview, she was providing very heavy care to her bed-ridden husband, who was near death. She spoke at length about the inter-connection between her emotional reactions to her mother's death and to her husband's approaching death. She felt that she has not accepted her mother's death but that she will be able to do so once her husband dies:

> I don't think I fully accepted it. Uhm—what I really think is that when my husband goes, I'll just kind of have this big—explosion. Maybe after that [sobs], I'll accept it. (63, DA/MO)

Intimacy and Caregiving

This theme emerged in the supporting statements of both accepting and non-accepting respondents and was associated with both claims in various ways. For example, several respondents grounded their acceptance in the care they provided for their parent. Others accepted the death with gratitude as a relief from the caregiving obligation. A few respondents could not accept their parent's death because it had robbed them of the opportunity to provide that care.

For some respondents, caregiving provided an opportunity for intimacy with the parent that was profoundly meaningful. It allowed them to return the physical care to the parent that the parent had offered them as an infant and child. Most important, however, it appeared to provide respondents with the opportunity to accompany their parent to the door of death, permitting them in a few cases to literally hold their mother or father in their arms as the parent died, and in others permitting the parent to die at home, surrounded by family members. For these respondents, a personal conviction that they had achieved an otherwise impossible intimacy with their parent led to their acceptance of their parent's death.

> Well, like I say, you go through all this trauma with him. And-uh-not only this, but you look back at the past, and all [he did for you]. And you say to yourself: I don't want to leave him now, you know, in his last—his last—you know. (Right. Right.) Even though it sounds cruel, I wanted to see him take his last breath. It's because of what I've been through with him. And I just feel that if I wasn't there when he died, I would have lost a lot. I could accept it a lot easier considering the fact that he was here with us. (65, SO/FA)

> Well, I feel like I have accepted her death, only because—like—uh—. She continually apologized that we had to put her on the commode: "Well, *that's* a shame. I can do it myself! You don't have to do it." I said: "Mom, don't worry about it. You know we want to do it." I said: "How about all the times *you* took care of *me*? Now, *I* want to take care of *you*." "Well, if that's the way you look at it—." I said: "Mom, that's the way I look at it." I said: "Look at all *I* been through." I said: "*You* were always there for *me*." (57, DA/MO)

For non-accepting respondents, however, the period of caregiving did not become a source of acceptance, but rather is now experienced as a source of profound emptiness that makes acceptance impossible. This daughter explained her non-acceptance by reporting an oft-spoken exchange with her mother:

> Uhm—there's a void, because I knew that I was on call, so to speak. Mother would call and say: Ada, I need this at the store, I need that at the store, and on your way up, stop at the—! And I would always say: Mother, now remember. You told me to stop at the store, so don't worry. Don't expect me 'til you see

me. Don't expect me to be there at a certain time. [Shrugs shoulders, breaking into silent tears] So. (62, DA/MO)

Similarly, another daughter explained that her father's death had not ended her thinking and planning about his care, but had only created a "dark and lonely" emptiness in which she is not needed:

Unh-unh, [no]. I CAN'T BELIEVE IT! [Voice breaks] Like, I'm still thinking: Oh, well. I have to go fix Daddy's pills. I got to make dinner for Daddy. I have to fix his medicine. Oh! He has to get up for his medicine. Oh! It's time for his medicine. Oh! It's time for his inhaler. And I look, and the house is so dark and lonely. And I think: What am I doing? Am I cracking up, you know? Am I really losing it?

And my sister did the same thing. Oh! What am I going to bring up for dinner for Daddy, she used to say. And then, you know, it would hit her. It was hard. (46, DA/FA)

Finally, caregiving was not regarded as an opportunity for intimacy by some respondents who articulated this theme. Rather, the parent's death brought a welcome relief from the need to give care, which the respondent regarded as a burden. This relief represented an important component of their acceptance:

Yes, I do [accept] it, 'cause—for her sake. I feel real good about it, matter of fact. I can't see suffering. And plus, it's a burden on everyone else. (What was?) I mean, God! (You were all working hard to take care of her?) Exactly. It's—it's just so tough, God! (50, SO/MO)

95% accepted. Every now and then there is a twinge in me that says: I don't want it to be this way. [But] to me, it's a relief. [Pause] To me, it makes my life easier. (By accepting?) NO! His being dead makes my life easier. Not that I would have wished him to be dead, to make my life easier. (44, SO/FA)

The Relationship between Acceptance Claims and Explanations: The Connectives

Assertions of acceptance or non-acceptance and the explanations that support them do not simply float in proximity to each other. Rather, a connected and meaningful relationship exists between them. The nature of the relationship can be characterized by considering the meaning of the word that links them, and those meanings are readily accessible through the sociolinguistic technique of semantic expansion. *Because* and *but* will occupy the present discussion, although other connectives do of course appear in acceptance talk. However, *because* and *but* are the most frequently occurring of the connectives and are centrally important in linking claims to thematic statements.

In technical linguistic terms, *because* is a causative conjunction. It signals a simple, causal relationship between the two statements that it conjoins [44-46]. In acceptance statements, *because* communicates a straightforward, causal link between acceptance (or non-acceptance) claims and the following explanations. For many respondents, the beliefs or values they articulate in their explanatory statements, or which are implicit in them, directly cause them to accept their parent's death.

Because appears most frequently, although not exclusively, as the linking word in acceptance talk that articulates themes of death's factuality. For example, the content of the following quotations reflects this theme and illustrates the causal meaning of this linking word:

> I did accept it *because* he isn't here, and I know that he can't be here. (43, DA/FA)

> I've accepted it *because* that's the way it's—that's the way it is. (42, DA/FA)

Similarly, *because* also appears frequently as a connective in explanatory statements that articulate the Natural Order theme:

> I accepted my father's death, *because* I know everybody has to die (60, SO/FA).

> Yeah, I have, *because*, like I said, it's the natural thing, OK? And this is—this is it. (40, SO/FA)

As we have seen, the element of death's factuality may also be expressed as spiritual belief, expressed with certainty as knowledge, among respondents who say they believe that death was God's will for their parent. For these adult children, the knowledge of God's will is as certain a fact as is others' knowledge of the physical fact of death. The use of *because* clearly positions this knowledge as the reason for their acceptance:

> Accepted it, yes, *because* I know it was God's will. Had it not been His will, she would have been here now. (65, DA/MO)

Non-acceptance is also causally linked to observable, factual circumstances. In the following quotation, one daughter enumerates aspects of her own behavior that cause her to conclude that she has not accepted her mother's death:

> I haven't accepted it, 'cause—'cause—I still miss her. Like, I still haven't been able to get rid of her clothes. When I go in her room, it seems like I glance toward the bed. I just realize she's not coming back. (42, DA/MO)

The predominance of *because* as the linking word in this wide range of thematic material suggests that respondents are making an important connection between fact and acceptance, and that connection is a causal one. Respondents who articulate these themes appear to regard death as a factual occurrence, whether natural or divine in origin. For them, acceptance is *caused* by their understanding of the nature of death. The simple, straightforward relationship between acceptance and their parent's death is signaled neatly by the causative form.

The situation is quite different among respondents who articulate themes in which *but* predominates. In the earlier discussion of Strong Feelings and Parent as Memory themes, we saw that *but* communicates a contrastive or oppositional relationship between acceptance claims and the explanatory statements that follow. In fact, *but* appears most frequently as the linking word in acceptance talk that articulates these two themes.

The interpretation of *but*'s role in acceptance talk is grounded in the theory of grammatical meaning. In technical, linguistic terms, *but* is an adversative co-ordinating conjunction. This means, first, that it introduces statements about circumstances or conditions that contrast with or oppose what is expressed in the preceding statement [34, 40, 47]. Second, as a co-ordinating conjunction, *but* indicates that the conjoined statements are of equal weight; neither one is dependent on the other for its full meaning [35, 46]. This expansion of *but*'s semantic and grammatical meaning is more than a pedantic exercise. To the contrary, it draws attention to the layers of meaning that are implicit in acceptance talk and, in doing so, clarifies that meaning.

Among respondents who employ *but* in their articulation of these themes, acceptance is positioned as an adversative, or contrasting, set of conditions, namely their acknowledgment of death's factuality and their awareness of their own strong emotional state or a transformation of their parent into memory. Acceptance is not caused by these conditions. Rather, acceptance co-exists in an almost adversarial relation with these other inner emotional or memory states. Attention to the semantic complexity of this linking word forces us to follow the adult child's shifting focus from one reality of his or her experience, i.e., a ready claim of acceptance or an acknowledgment of death's factuality, to another, contrasting reality, i.e., to strong emotions of sadness, anger or longing or to the parent's new life in the child's heart or mind.

Each part of the acceptance talk structure reveals an important aspect of acceptance. In the claim, respondents have a ready response to any inquiry about acceptance. In the statements that follow, respondents articulate a complexity of feelings and thoughts implicitly germane to their experience of acceptance. In the connecting words, respondents make explicit the way in which these feelings and thoughts are related to their claims. As competent speakers of the language, respondents adroitly utilize the resources of their grammar to communicate delicate balances between cognitive and emotional states, and to link these to overt claims of acceptance or non-acceptance. Sensitivity to the structural form that acceptance discourse takes and to the meaning of specific words offers valuable insight into this balance.

IMPLICATIONS AND DISCUSSION

Two findings emerge from these data. First, respondents regard their acceptance of parent death as directly following from their values and beliefs about the nature of death or as existing in tandem with powerful feelings and memories. Second, acceptance appears to be a phenomenon that respondents feel compelled to explain. Let us consider these findings in turn.

Beliefs about Death and the Power of Feeling

Acceptance is not foremost in the minds of these respondents as they discuss their bereavement. Only a few respondents introduce the word or topic themselves. They appear to find the term "acceptance" unfamiliar. Yet, when they are asked how the notion of acceptance might be applicable to their own situation, they are, in a manner of speaking, off and running. What respondents say about acceptance as it relates to their own experience differs significantly from much of what has been reported in the bereavement literature to date.

When data-based studies of adult children's reaction to parent death take up the issue of acceptance, they tend to relate acceptance to several factors. For example, acceptance is most frequently related to the reduction of overt symptoms of emotional distress [9, 10, 16, 48, 49]. Some studies relate acceptance of the death to the parent/child relationship, but typically report contradictory findings. For example, acceptance of the death is related to parent/child closeness [16], parent/child distance [9], and independence from the parent/child tie [16], while non-acceptance of the death is related to closeness [48]. A few studies consider acceptance in the context of the length of the parent's illness and the length of the actual dying. Here, studies report more consistent findings in that greater acceptance is related to the adult child's perception that the parent's death came in a timely manner after a lengthy illness or protracted dying [9, 18].

In contrast, the data presented in this analysis indicate that acceptance of parent death is related to the adult child's beliefs about the very nature of death rather than the factors mentioned above. Affirmative claims are directly linked to and explained by beliefs about death's factuality, immutability and naturalness or to the certain knowledge of death as God's will. Strong feelings of sadness or longing for the parent and powerful transformations of the parent into memory do not displace acceptance, but rather contextualize it or co-occur with it. Claims of non-acceptance are not related to any of the factors most commonly identified in the literature. Rather, non-accepting respondents relate their denials to their own behavior that maintains interaction with the deceased parent, to family behaviors that interfere with acceptance, and to interpretations of the parent's medical care as unacceptable.

The sons and daughters in this study do not discuss their acceptance in terms of cessation of crying, returned appetites, or the reduction of other depressive symptoms. Neither do they relate their acceptance to the emotional closeness or distance between themselves and their parent. While the Parent as Memory theme comes closest to such considerations, note that its focus is on the transformation of the parent as an individual character and identity into memory, rather than the relationship between the child and the parent. Similarly, while aspects of the Caregiving and Intimacy theme may superficially seem to reflect the parent/child tie, the focus of this thematic material is primarily on one shared activity in the last year of the parent's life rather than the sum total of the parent/child history.

Only notions of timeliness reported in the literature appear to find parallels in these respondents' discussion of their acceptance, specifically in the Death as Endpoint theme. As respondents have articulated this theme, death figures as an understood, often welcome, end to some trajectory in the parent's life, either to a lengthy illness, a lengthy dying, a lengthy relationship or a lengthy life.

In sum, this analysis offers new insights into how adult sons and daughters understand and interpret the causes and conditions of their acceptance.

Explaining Acceptance

The most compelling finding of this study, in my view, is that respondents almost categorically offer an explanation for their acceptance. Whether affirmed or denied, on whatever grounds, acceptance is an experience that most sons and daughters feel they must somehow explain. We have examined the content of their explanations, but the fact of explanation-giving itself remains to be accounted for. What is it about the acceptance of an elderly parent's death that requires such explanation?

In attempting to answer this question, we must first consider whether or not the explained nature of acceptance is inherent in the phenomenon itself or whether it is an artifact of the interview structure. Is it a naturally occurring discourse structure that represents almost all respondents' experiences of the reality of acceptance? Or, does it result from the question/answer format constraints of the research interview?

We could argue that the question/answer structure of the research interview elicits a yes/no reply and subsequent talk that elaborates on the reply. In the effort to appear as a competent individual, the respondent presents his or her experience of acceptance as a rational, orderly account rather than as the diffuse or irrelevant experience it may really be.

There are important counter-arguments to be made, which, in my view, strongly suggest that acceptance is a phenomenon that must, for some reason, be explained. First, the wording of the question offered much latitude for individual reaction. The respondent is not forced into a yes/no response by directly asking: "Have you or haven't you accepted your parent's death?" The form of the query acknowledges the likely range of response, first, by raising the possibility and expectation that different experiences will be communicated (i.e., "some say . . . others say . . .") and, second, that the reaction of the individual respondent may differ form all others (i.e., "How was it for you?")

Second, although follow-up probing was rarely necessary for this question, when it was required, interview techniques were employed that avoided direct elicitation. For example, a respondent was not asked for a reason for her or his claim of acceptance, such as "Why or why not?" Rather, the technique of repeating back the response to the respondent was adopted [7, 50]. For example, "You accepted your mother's death" or the standard assent term "Mmmh-hmmmhm" was offered to whatever was said as encouragement to continue.

Third, preliminary analyses of the structure of spontaneously introduced acceptance discourse is identical to the discourse structure we have been considering at length in our discussion. If acceptance were not an intrinsically accountable experience, we would expect to see spontaneous acceptance discourse take another shape. It does not.

Fourth, other equally difficult and powerful topics do not elicit explanations such as those offered for acceptance. For example, questions about anticipatory grief, perceptions of personal finitude or comparative reactions to other deaths which might well elicit lengthy explanations because of their complexity and evanescence do not do so.

Finally, the discourse structure that we have been considering, i.e., claim + connective + explanatory statements, was uniform for all respondents represented in the study, irrespective of age, social-class, ethnicity, quality of the parent/child tie, accepting or not accepting of the death.

Accordingly, if we accept the explanatory tone of the acceptance response as inherent in the response itself rather than in the interview structure, we return to the question: what is it about the acceptance of an elderly parent's death that requires such an explanation? In my view, the answer lies in the role explanation plays in acceptance talk.

Earlier, it was suggested that the structure of acceptance talk strongly resembles the structure of discourse units such as vernacular arguments, accounts or disclaimers whose role is to support positions articulated by participants in the social exchange. For example, Schiffrin contends that in vernacular argument, when a speaker advocates a controversial proposition, he or she quickly follows that proposition with reasoned support for the position [34]. Similarly, symbolic interactionists argue that when disruptions occur in the micro-web of norms and attitudes that organize and support face-to-face interaction, the perpetrator of the infraction quickly reorganizes and repairs the offense via a disclaimer (28-29) of responsibility or an explanation for how such an offense could have occurred [28-31].

Building on this perspective, then, I propose that this is exactly how acceptance talk functions for the respondents represented in this study. Specifically, the respondent regards the claim of acceptance, whether affirmed or denied, as an infraction or a violation of some belief or value which must then be redressed. The redress takes the form of the statements respondents offer to support their acceptance claim.

But what belief or value has been compromised? Without the support of ethnographically sensitive analyses of grief, we can only speculate. However, the bereavement literature on parent death typically characterizes the death of a parent as normative [51-55], and argues that the bereavement associated with it is likely to be less intense than for other deaths because of its normative character. Although this characterization of parent death is not, to my knowledge, supported by any ethnography, it is widely articulated in the literature, and may reflect a generalized, cultural belief to which the participants in our study also have access. Indeed, as we have seen in the discussion of the Death as Endpoint theme, some respondents do link their perception of parent death as a normative experience to their acceptance.

Let us speculate, then, that respondents hold in their minds the idea that their parent's death is an event they will most likely have to face in their middle or later years. While they expect that they will be emotionally touched by the death, they do not anticipate being emotionally decimated, because, after all, it is a normative death. Yet, when the elderly mother or father dies, emotional turmoil surrounds the death. The normalcy of the death is not the mitigating factor the middle-aged child expected it to be. The adult child finds himself or herself having emotions that appear to be at variance with what he or she had expected. The respondent is thus confronted with cultural expectations and emotional experience that conflict.

At present, we can again only speculate about where the conflict lies. Several scenarios can be envisioned. On the one hand, for example, by claiming to accept the death, a son or daughter betrays the reality of the emotional reaction that the loss of the parent engenders. On the other hand, a strong emotional experience violates the cultural value that (perhaps comfortingly) predicts a mitigated reaction to the death. Still further, a denial of acceptance, while recognizing the strength and reality of the emotional reaction, undercuts the very premise that supports the conventional belief, i.e., that it is normal for an adult child's elderly parent to die and normal for the adult child to feel *less* rather than *more* about that death.

In my view, the explanation we identify in acceptance talk is respondents' effort to make sense of their conflicting expectations and experiences. An explanation, an account, is what emerges out of the confusion about what they believe they ought to feel, what they do feel, and what the conflict is felt to signify. The explanatory nature of acceptance discourse is a reflection of an inner dialogue in which bereaved daughters and sons struggle to make sense of the collision between the normative expectations they have internalized and their actual experience of their parent's death.

Understanding acceptance talk as explanation points to the respondent's experience of a tiny tear somewhere in the web of beliefs and values that he or she holds about his or her parent's death. The explanation is aimed at repairing that tear. For the majority of respondents, the conflict is resolved by reference to their certain knowledge about the factuality, the immutability, the naturalness of death and their knowledge of God's will. For others, the power of their own feelings and memories exists in tandem with their acceptance.

REFERENCES

1. E. Lindeman, Symptomatology and Management of Acute Grief, *American Journal of Psychiatry, 101*, pp. 141-148, 1944.
2. C. Parkes, *Bereavement*, International Universities Press, New York, 1972.
3. J. Bowlby, *Loss: Sadness and Depression. Volume III of Attachment and Loss*, Basic Books, New York, 1980.
4. J. W. Worden, *Grief Counseling and Grief Therapy*, Springer Publishing Co., New York, 1982.
5. J. Stephensen, *Death, Grief and Mourning: Individual and Social Realities*, Free Press, New York, 1985.
6. M. Angel, *The Orphaned Adult: Confronting the Death of a Parent*, Human Sciences Press, New York, 1987.
7. D. Berardo, Bereavement and Mourning, in *Dying: Facing the Facts*, H. Wass, F. Berardo, and R. Neimeyer (eds.), Hemisphere Publishing Corp., Washington, D.C., pp. 279-300, 1988.
8. R. Weiss, Loss and Recovery, *Journal of Social Issues, 44*:3, pp. 37-52, 1988.
9. R. Kerr, Meanings Adult Daughters Attach to a Parent's Death, *Western Journal of Nursing Research, 16*:4, pp. 347-365, 1994.
10. J. Leahy, A Comparison of Depression in Women Bereaved of a Spouse, Child or a Parent, *Omega, 26*:3, pp. 207-217, 1993.
11. T. Rando, *Grieving*, Ballantine Books, New York, 1988.
12. S. Schuchter and S. Zisook, The Course of Normal Grief, in *Handbook of Bereavement: Theory, Research and Intervention*, M. Stroebe, W. Stroebe, and R. Hansson (eds.), Cambridge University Press, New York, pp. 23-43, 1993.
13. M. Stroebe, W. Stroebe, and R. Hansson, *Handbook of Bereavement: Theory, Research and Intervention*, M. Stroebe, W. Stroebe, and R. Hansson (eds.), Cambridge University Press, New York, 1993.
14. C. Wortman, R. Silver, and R. Kessler, The Meaning of Loss and Adjustment to Bereavement, in *Handbook of Bereavement: Theory, Research and Intervention*, M. Stroebe, W. Stroebe, and R. Hansson (eds.), Cambridge University Press, New York, pp. 349-366, 1993.

15. S. Shuchter, *Dimensions of Grief: Adjusting to the Death of a Spouse*, Jossey-Bass, San Francisco, 1986.
16. P. Popek and A. Scharlach, Adult Daughters' Relationship with Their Mothers and Reactions to Mothers' Deaths, *Journal of Women and Aging*, 3:4, pp. 79-95, 1991.
17. C. Wortman and R. Silver, The Myths of Coping with Loss, *The Journal of Consulting and Clinical Psychology*, 57:3, pp. 349-357, 1989.
18. M. Moss, S. Moss, R. Rubinstein, and N. Resch, Impact of Elderly Mother's Death on Middle Age Daughters, *International Journal of Aging and Human Development*, 37:1, pp. 1-20, 1992.
19. G. White, Emotions Inside and Out: The Anthropology of Affect, in *Handbook of Emotions*, M. Lewis and J. Havilland (eds.), Guilford Press, New York, pp. 29-39, 1993.
20. D. Middleton, Emotional Style: The Cultural Ordering of Emotions, *Ethos*, pp. 187-201, 1987.
21. C. Lutz and G. White, The Anthropology of Emotions, *Annual Review of Anthropology (15)*, Annual Reviews Inc., Palo Alto, California, pp. 405-436, 1986.
22. G. White and J. Kirkpatrick, *Person, Self and Experience: Exploring Pacific Ethnopsychologies*, University of California Press, Berkeley, 1985.
23. D. Holland and A. Kipnis, Metaphors for Embarrassment and Stories of Exposure: The Not-So-Egocentric Self in American Culture, *Ethos*, 22:3, pp. 316-342, 1994.
24. C. Lutz and L. Abu-Lughod, *Language and the Politics of Emotion*, Cambridge University Press, Cambridge, 1989.
25. L. Abu-Lughod, *Veiled Sentiments: Honor and Poetry in a Bedouin Society*, University of California Press, Berkeley, 1986.
26. E. Schieffelin, Anger, Grief and Shame: Toward a Kaluli Ethnopsychiatry, in *In Person, Self and Experience: Exploring Pacific Ethnopsychologies*, G. White and J. Kirkpatrick (eds.), University of California Press, Berkeley, pp. 168-182, 1985.
27. R. Rosaldo, Grief and the Headhunter's Rage: On the Cultural Force of Emotion, in *Text, Play and Story: The Construction and Reconstruction of Self and Society*, E. Bruner (ed.), Waveland Press, Prospect Heights, Illinois, pp. 178-195, 1984.
28. M. Scott and S. Lyman, Accounts, *American Sociological Review*, 33, pp. 46-62, 1968.
29. R. Stokes and J. Hewitt, Aligning Actions, *American Sociological Review*, 41, pp. 383-449, 1976.
30. M. Cody and M. McLaughlin, Models for the Sequential Construction of Accounting Episodes: Situational and Interactional Constraints on Message Selection and Evaluation, in *Sequence and Pattern in Communicative Behavior*, R. Street and J. Cappella (eds.), Edward Arnold, New York, pp. 50-69, 1985.
31. C. Heath, The Delivery and Reception of Diagnosis in the General Practice Consultation, in *Talk at Work: Interaction in Institutional Settings*, P. Drew and J. Heritage (eds.), Cambridge University Press, Cambridge, pp. 235-267, 1992.
32. J. Hewitt and R. Stokes, Disclaimers, *American Sociological Review*, 40:1, pp. 1-11, 1975.

33. R. Hopper, J. Ward, W. Thompson, and P. Sias, Two Types of Institutional Disclaimers at the Cancer Information Service, in *The Talk of the Clinic: Explorations in the Analysis of Medical and Therapeutic Discourse*, G. Morris and R. Chenail (eds.), Lawrence Erlbaum Associates, Hillsdale, New Jersey, pp. 171-184, 1995.
34. D. Schiffren, *Discourse Markers*, Cambridge University Press, London, 1987.
35. W. Labov, *Sociolinguistic Patterns*, University of Pennsylvania Press, Philadelphia, 1972.
36. M. Luborsky, Identifying Themes and Patterns, in *Qualitative Methods in Aging Research*, J. Gubrium and A. Sankar (eds.), Sage Publications, New York, pp. 175-194, 1994.
37. M. Luborsky and R. Rubinstein, Sampling in Qualitative Research: Rationale, Issues, Methods, *Research on Aging*, (forthcoming).
38. J. Gumperz, *Discourse Strategies*, Cambridge University Press, Cambridge, 1982.
39. E. Traugott and M. Pratt, *Linguistics for Students of Literature*, Harcourt, Brace, Jovanovitch, New York, 1980.
40. D. Tannen, *Framing in Discourse*, Oxford University Press, London, 1993.
41. W. Labov and D. Fanshel, *Therapeutic Discourse: Psychotherapy as Conversation*, Academic Press, New York, 1977.
42. H. Black, R. Rubinstein, and M. Goodman, *Spiritual Performance in Older Men*, paper presented at Gerontological Association of America Annual Meeting in Los Angeles, California, 1995.
43. J. Livingston, *Anatomy of the Sacred*, Macmillan Press, New York, 1987.
44. R. Quirk, S. Greenbaum, G. Leech, and J. Svartvik, *A Grammar of Contemporary English*, Longman Press, London, 1979.
45. G. Leech and J. Svartvik, *A Communicative Grammar of English*, Longman Group, London, 1975.
46. C. Onions, *Modern English Syntax*, St. Martin's Press, New York, 1974.
47. C. Peterson and A. McCabe, *Developing Narrative Structure*, Lawrence Erlbaum Associates, Hillsdale, New Jersey, 1991.
48. J. Douglas, Patterns of Change Following Parent Death in Midlife Adults, *Omega*, 22:2, pp. 123-137, 1990-91.
49. A. Scharlach and K. Fredriksen, Reactions to the Death of a Parent during Midlife, *Omega*, 27:4, pp. 307-319, 1993.
50. J. Matarazzo, Interviewer mm-hmmm and Interview Speech Duration, *Psychotherapy: Theory, Research and Practice*, 1, pp. 109-114, 1964.
51. R. Kastenbaum, Death and Development through the Lifespan, in *New Meanings of Death*, H. Feifel (eds.), McGraw-Hill, New York, pp. 17-45, 1977.
52. M. Moss and S. Moss, The Impact of Parental Death on Middle-Aged Children, *Omega*, 14:1, pp. 65-75, 1983-84.
53. M. Moss and S. Moss, The Death of a Parent, in *Midlife Loss: Coping Strategies*, R. Kalish (ed.), Sage, Newbury Park, California, pp. 89-114, 1989.
54. B. Dane, Middle Aged Adults Mourning the Death of a Parent, *Journal of Gerontological Social Work*, 14:3/4, pp. 75-89, 1989.

55. M. Moss and S. Moss, Death and Bereavement, in *Handbook of Aging and the Family*, R. Blieszner and V. Bedford (eds.), Greenwood Press, Westport, Connecticut, pp. 422-439, 1995.

LONG-TERM PSYCHOLOGICAL AND SOMATIC CONSEQUENCES OF LATER LIFE PARENTAL BEREAVEMENT*

BRIAN DE VRIES, PH.D.
University of British Columbia and
San Francisco State University, California

CHRISTOPHER G. DAVIS, PH.D.
University of British Columbia and
Institute for Social Research, University of Michigan

CAMILLE B. WORTMAN, PH.D.
State University of New York, Stony Brook

DARRIN R. LEHMAN, PH.D.
University of British Columbia

ABSTRACT

The death of an adult child is purported to precipitate the most distressing and long-lasting of all grief reactions. The empirical literature surrounding such a claim, however, is primarily clinical and anecdotal in nature with relatively arbitrary and small samples. Drawing from a nationally representative sample of adults (Americans' Changing Lives, 1986, 1989), we examine the long-term effects of the death of an adult child longitudinally over two waves of assessment separated by two and one-half years. The bereaved sample comprised seventy-seven parents (78% female) with a mean age of approximately seventy years whose adult child (mean age at time of death was 42 years) had

---

*Portions of this research were reported at the meeting of the Gerontological Association of America, New Orleans, Louisiana, 1993. Preparation of this manuscript was facilitated by the awarding of a Social Sciences and Humanities Research Council of Canada (SSHRCC) grant to the first author and a SSHRCC graduate fellowship to the second author. Data collection was supported by a series of National Institute of Aging grants to J. S. House, R. C. Kessler, and C. B. Wortman.

© 1997, Baywood Publishing Co., Inc.

died within the preceding one to ten years. Results indicated that, in comparison with a comparably aged group of non-bereaved parents, the bereaved group experienced higher levels of depression. Additionally, the bereaved group reported slightly higher levels of marital satisfaction and expressed somewhat different sources of life satisfaction and different sources of worry. From Wave 1 to Wave 2 of assessment, health status declined at a more rapid rate for the bereaved than the control and the higher levels of depression for the bereaved did not change. Discussion focuses on the meaning of the death of a child, and an adult child in particular, and the complexity of the associated bereavement process.

A child's death has been described as life's greatest tragedy and an existential wound [1]—a violation of the natural order of the universe [2]. The consequent parental bereavement reflects the magnitude of this loss and is said to be "severe, complicated and long lasting" [3, p. xi] and resistant to the effects of time [4]. These strong claims frame the study reported herein: an examination of the psychological and self-perceived physical health of older parents bereft of an adult child between one to ten years. In significant advances over previous research, two assessment periods, separated by almost three years, are included as is a comparison group of non-bereaved adults of a similar age range to address adaptation independent of the "normative" effects of aging.

BACKGROUND

Although there exists an expanding and moderately impressive body of research on the effects of a child's death on parents, much remains to be discovered [5]. Klass and Marwit have claimed that the complex reactions presented by parents following the death of a child are not adequately captured by the predominant view of bereavement [6]. This view also has been criticized more generally [e.g., 7, 8] for its focus on a prescribed endpoint of recovery and the chronological and linear process by which it is achieved and its relative overemphasis on widowhood [9]. When this endpoint is not attained, the effort is deemed to have failed and the individual is assumed to be experiencing deviant or pathological grief [e.g., 5].

In contrast, researchers report an intensification of *parental grief* over time [e.g., 3] with significant levels of depression even seven years following the death [10] and suggestions of "permanent effects on functioning and the inner lives of parents" [4, p. 298]. The intensity of parental grief has been attributed to the uniqueness of the parent-child relationship [3, 11] and the concomitant meanings and representations a child holds for the parent [12]; parental hopes, joys, sense of competence, responsibilities, efforts, and failures are manifested in and represented by the child [13]. The death is perceived as an assault on parents' sense of continuity—a severance of the link between the past and the future [12] and the loss of a parent's "immortality project" [14]. Parents perceive their role as ending with their death, not the death of their child [15].

It has been suggested that the meanings and responses to deaths in general and the death of a child in particular may be further informed by a life course perspective [3, 9, 13, 16]. For example, later life has been characterized as a time of multiple personal, health, and social losses [e.g., 17]—all perceived as intimations of an individual's mortality [18]. In this light, an adult child's death is seen as an especially dissynchronous event [2, 19] for the parents were "next in line" to die. Thus, the impact of the death of a child may be even greater for parental survivors in later life [11] in which adjustments to the loss is further complicated and exacerbated by the longevity of relationships with affectively richer memories [20] and a concomitant intertwining of lives [21]. Gorer's interviews with six bereft parents have yielded perhaps the most often-quoted comment in this literature and reflects this view: "The most distressing and long-lasting of all griefs, it would seem, is that of the loss of a grown child" [22, p. 121].

Enhanced by the writings of Klass and Marwit [6], among others, and the relative incongruence with the general bereavement literature of the above data and observations on the experiences of the bereft, there has been a recent appreciation of the multidimensionality of bereavement reactions [23] that appear in "the movement to recovery" [24]. Prominent among these dimensions are psychological and somatic distress [4]. These dimensions organize the brief literature review that follows, highlighting the reports on older bereft parents, and structure the research reported herein.

THE PSYCHOLOGICAL CONSEQUENCES OF LATER LIFE PARENTAL BEREAVEMENT

The history of the study of parental bereavement in the later years has primarily anecdotal and clinical roots with frequent reference to Freud's differentiation of mourning (i.e., normal grief) from melancholia (i.e., chronic depression) [25]. The interpretations of these collective works have led directly to examinations of the grief and depression evidenced by bereft parents. For example, slightly more than two years following the accidental death of an adult child, Shanfield and Swain [26] found that parents continued to grieve intensely, a finding echoed by Videka-Sherman and Lieberman [27]. Lesher and Bergey found significant grief reactions and levels of clinical depression in the eighteen institutionalized mothers they studied an average of six years following their child's death [28].

This grief and depression have assumed several forms. Rubin [29], for example, reported greater despair, depersonalization, rumination, and somatization for the older parents in his study; Fish found evidence of isolation, loss of control, death anxiety, and anger among the parents he studied [30]. Feelings of guilt also are reported to be characteristic of later life parental bereavement [26,

29] as are high levels of anxiety even up to thirteen years following the loss [31]. Florian reported that regardless of the time since the death, older bereaved parents demonstrated significantly less meaning and purpose in life than a non-bereaved comparison group [32]. This lack of meaning was evident in work, in coping with problems and in feelings of uselessness, perhaps interpretable in terms of a more general change in orientation to life as a consequence of loss.

Several diffuse yet related effects have been reported, together reflecting aspects of the general context within which the loss is experienced. For example, framed in terms of the life course, Rubin found that older parents manifested more depressive symptoms than did younger parents in response to the death of an adult son [29]. Along comparable lines, Fish reported that older fathers experienced greater grief than younger fathers although there were no age differences in the grief experiences of mothers [30]. In the context of gender and family roles, Shanfield and Swain reported that the death of an adult daughter produced the greatest grief response for both parents [26]. Arbuckle and de Vries, in a comparison of spousally and parentally bereaved, reported several gender differences, although these tended to be uninfluenced by loss type; they interpret these "main effects" as evidence of the socio-historical context within which (older) grievers have been socialized [9]. In summary, the long-term effects of later life parental bereavement appear to be significant and persistent and include depression and generalized psychological distress further influenced (or perhaps represented) by the context within which the loss takes place.

THE SOMATIC CONSEQUENCES OF LATER LIFE PARENTAL BEREAVEMENT

Several studies suggest that physical health problems may remain evident over the long-term course of adjustment for parents who have suffered the death of an adult child. For example, when compared with non-bereaved parents of similar ages, Florian found poorer perceived health among bereaved parents [32]. Lesher and Bergey found that the elderly bereaved mothers of their sample reported health difficulties associated with insomnia and nervousness and that hip or other bone fractures had doubled since bereavement [28]. The bereaved parents (and mothers especially) in the Shanfield and Swain study similarly reported more health complaints since the accidental death of their adult child [26]. Shanfield, Benjamin, and Swain compared older parents whose children died accidentally with parents whose children died from cancer [33]. They found that parents who had experienced a sudden, accidental death reported greater health problems than parents who had experienced an expected loss, suggesting that cause of death, and/or perhaps relationships prior to death, may be a mitigating factor affecting physical health.

Several studies have examined war-related loss specifically. For example, in a study comparing parents bereft of an adult child with non-bereft controls, Levav reported a significantly higher mortality rate among the bereaved [34]. In a subsequent study, Levav, Friedlander, Kark, and Peritz compared parents whose sons died in war with parents whose sons died of accidental causes and revealed more complex differences [35]. Overall, no elevated mortality rate was noted although, interestingly, spouseless parents evidenced a higher age-adjusted mortality rate than married parents perhaps attributable to factors of bereavement overload [36] and/or diminished social resources.

In a study examining health effects ten years following the death, Rubin compared older parents who had lost an adult son in war with middle-aged parents who had lost a younger child [29]. Both at the initial time of death and ten years after the loss, the retrospective data indicated that older parents experienced more physical health difficulties in the form of greater degree of sleep disturbances, appetite problems and other physical health symptoms (some of which may be the physical manifestations of depression) than did younger parents. These problems subsided over the long-term course of bereavement, although Rubin reported that these difficulties did not disappear completely. The absence of a control group leaves open the possibility that these difficulties may reflect age-related health deterioration.

A related report by Rubin compared older parents bereft of an adult child through war as much as thirteen years previously with a comparison group of parents whose adult child had left or was leaving home [4]. Results generally revealed affective, cognitive, and somatic effects that differentiated the bereft from the non-bereft and were relatively independent of time since loss. In summary, past data suggest that later life parental bereavement is associated with significant deleterious effects on health over which time has little influence.

STUDY OBJECTIVES

The foregoing review suggests significant and long-lasting psychological and somatic consequences of parental bereavement in later life. As previously mentioned, however, several sampling and methodological problems qualify many of these results. In particular, samples often have been homogeneous, small and select [28, 34], frequently drawn from special bereavement (self-help) groups or clinical populations. The results on long-term adjustment often are derived from cross-sectional and retrospective data, mandating caution in interpretation. Moreover, respondents generally have been recruited on the basis of their special status as bereaved and are informed of the study purposes and goals prior to participation (see [10] for a detailed discussion of this issue; also see [2]). With refusal rates often in excess of 50 percent, it is unclear the extent to which those who participate are representative of the bereaved in general. Control or comparison groups are surprisingly rare, and when included, many sociodemographic factors have been left to vary. The instruments used have also varied greatly, often created for the purposes of the investigation making comparisons across studies difficult and of questionable validity.

The Americans' Changing Lives survey (ACL; a large, 2-wave national probability sample of non-institutionalized American adults) offers an unique opportunity to address many of these methodological and sampling criticisms while at the same time explore some of the defining issues of parental bereavement in the later years. For example, the long-term effects of later life parental bereavement on both psychological and physical health, independent of the effects of aging, may be examined with this longitudinal data set. Additionally, the socio-historical, demographic, and familial context (i.e., age, gender, education, income, race, marital status, and number of children) within which bereavement occurs—an often omitted and neglected aspect in the bereavement process [9, 37]—may be better controlled and accounted for with these data. The sample for ACL (from which the bereaved parents and their comparisons are drawn) comprise adults who were invited to participate in a large survey on health, stress, and productive activity over the life course [38].

METHOD

Respondents

The first wave of ACL was conducted in 1986. To be eligible to participate at that time, respondents had to be at least twenty-five years of age and residing in non-institutionalized housing in the continental United States. The sample was designed to represent a cross-section of Americans, although African Americans and persons over sixty were over-sampled. The follow-up wave of the study was conducted in 1989.

Respondents participating in both waves of the probability sample who indicated in the Wave 1 (1986) interview that they were bereaved of an adult child within the preceding ten years represented our bereaved sample. (For our purposes, we define an adult child as at least twenty years of age.) The control sample comprised participants who were 1) parents, 2) not bereaved of a child, 3) within the same age range, and 4) race as the bereaved parents.

Response Rates and Attrition

Face-to-face interviews were conducted with 3614 respondents in 1986. The overall response rate at wave 1 was 76 percent. Five percent ($n = 181$) of the sample indicated that they had lost a child (of any age) since 1976. Twelve of these bereaved parents (i.e., 6.6%) died before the second interview. Twenty-eight bereaved parents (15.5%) could not be located or declined to participate in the second interview in 1989, leaving an eligible bereaved sample of 141. The attrition rate for the bereaved sample was identical to that for the non-bereaved (Chi-square = 0.00). The bereaved parents' mortality rate was slightly, but not significantly, higher than that of those participants who were not bereaved of a child (4%; Chi-square = 2.25, $df = 1$, $p < .15$).

Of the 141 bereaved parents participating in both interviews, thirty-six had lost a child younger than twenty years of age. Of the remaining 105 bereaved parents, twenty-one reported that another child of theirs had died between the two interviews,[1] and seven provided inconsistent data across the two waves with respect to their deceased child (i.e., reporting at wave 2 that they had never lost a child or describing the loss of a different child than the one reported at wave 1). These cases were excluded from the analyses that follow, thus leaving a final bereaved sample of seventy-seven parents.

Since all of the seventy-seven bereaved parents were either African American or Caucasian, non-bereaved parents who were neither were selected out of the control sample. As well, since all but one of the seventy-seven parents were at least fifty years of age, the control sample was restricted to those at least fifty years of age. This left a control sample of 998 non-bereaved parents.

Information Regarding the Deceased

The mean age of the deceased child at the time of death was 42.1 years ($SD = 10.8$). Ages ranged from twenty-one to sixty-three years. The mean time since the death (from the first interview in 1986) was 3.9 years ($SD = 3.0$), with a range of one to ten years. Sixty-five percent of the children who died were male. Eleven parents (14.3%) lost their only child. In 66 percent of the cases, the death was described by the parent as unexpected. Table 1 summarizes the causes of death.

Interview Instrument

Four aspects of psychological and somatic adjustment were assessed. Depression was assessed with an eleven-item version of the Center for Epidemiological Studies Depression Scale (CES-D; [39]). On a 3-point scale, respondents indicated how often they experienced each depressive symptom during the past week. Higher scores thus indicate more depressive symptoms. Cronbach's alpha for the scale, averaged over the two interviews, was .79. Self-esteem was measured by three items taken from Rosenberg's [40] Self-esteem Scale. Respondents indicated the extent to which they agreed, using a 4-point scale (1 = "strongly agree," 4 = "strongly disagree"), with each statement (e.g., "I take a positive attitude

---

[1] These prospective data on the 21 parents who lost an additional child represent a unique opportunity to explore several neglected features of loss (including bereavement overload and relationships prior to death) and will be examined further and in greater detail in a subsequent report.

Table 1. Cause of Death of Adult Children
(N = 77)

Cause of Death	Percent
Cancer	24.7
Heart attack	26.0
Stroke	3.9
Other heart/blood problem	6.5
Motor vehicle accident	9.1
Industrial/work accident	2.6
Other accident	6.5
Suicide	5.2
Murder	1.3
Lung/respiratory prob. (exc. cancer)	2.6
Endocrine, metabolic, nutr. probs.	2.6
Neurological problem	1.3
Cirrhosis	1.3
Lupus	1.3
Other	1.3
Don't know	2.6
Missing	1.3

toward myself"; alpha = .56). Lower scores therefore represent greater self-esteem. Marital/Relationship satisfaction was measured by asking respondents who were married or living with a partner the extent to which they agreed or disagreed on the same 4-point scale with statements such as, "There is a great deal of love and affection expressed in our relationship" and "My (spouse/partner) doesn't treat me as well as I deserve to be treated" (reversed). Low scores represent greater marital satisfaction. Alphas for the scale at both waves of the interview were .83. Perceived health was assessed through two questions that measured respondents' self-ratings of their health (e.g., "How would you rate your health at the present time?"), in addition to a functional health index, which rated respondents in terms of their ability to perform daily tasks, ranging from bathing themselves to doing heavy work around their home. Higher scores indicate poorer perceived health; Alphas for the combined health measure was .79 at both interviews.

Early in the Wave 1 interview, respondents were asked, "At this stage in your life, what are your most important sources of satisfaction or pleasure?", followed by, "At this stage in your life, what are your most important problems, worries, or concerns?" Responses were later categorized into nine (mutually exclusive) sources of satisfaction and nine problems or worries. The nine sources of satisfaction were: family, work or education, assets or financial security, health (self, family, and friends), social relationships, leisure activities, religion, miscellaneous, and "no sources of satisfaction or pleasure." The nine categories of problems and worries were: family, work or education, assets or financial security, health, death (self, family, or friends), social relationships, leisure activities, miscellaneous, and "no problems or worries."

Recent Negative Life Experiences

In the first interview, respondents were asked if, during the past three years, they have been 1) widowed, 2) divorced, 3) the victim of a physical attack or assault, 4) involuntarily laid off or fired, 5) retired, or had experienced a 6) life-threatening, or 7) serious, but not life-threatening, illness or injury. In the second interview, respondents were asked if they had experienced these events since the first interview. The number of events that each respondent had experienced was summed to obtain a measure of the number of recent stressful experiences (excepting the loss of a child).

Self-Rated Recovery from the Child's Death

Respondents who indicated that a child of theirs had died were asked, "In general, how well do you feel you have dealt up to now with (his/her) death and any changes or problems which may have resulted from it?" Response categories ranged from (1) "Very well" to (4) "Not too well."

RESULTS

Demographics of the Samples

Despite the comparable age ranges, bereaved parents were nevertheless older on average ($M = 69.6$) than controls ($M = 65.2$; $t = 4.52, p < .001$). Seventy-eight percent of the bereaved parents were female compared to only 65.5 percent of the control group (Chi-square = 4.38, $df = 1, p < .05$). Forty-five percent of the bereaved sample was African American, compared with only 23 percent of the control sample (Chi-square = 18.14, $df = 1, p < .001$). Control respondents also were more educated ($M = 11.2$ years of education) than bereaved parents ($M = 9.9$ years; $t = 3.38, p = .001$). Bereaved parents reported a slightly lower family income ($M = \$18,600$) than controls ($M = \$23,500$; $t = 1.85, p < .10$).

Bereaved and control samples differed in terms of marital status (Chi-square = 10.92, $df = 4, p < .05$). Relative to controls, the bereaved parents were more likely to be widowed at the time of the 1986 interview (Bereaved parents: 41.6% widowed, Controls: 25.6%; Chi-square = 9.36, $df = 1, p < .005$), and, correspondingly, less likely to be married (Bereaved parents: 50.6% married, Controls: 63%; Chi-square = 4.56, $df = 1, p < .05$). On average, widows who were also bereaved of a child had been widowed 16.4 years prior to the first interview ($SD = 11.6$), whereas widows who were not bereaved of a child had been widowed 13.9 years ($SD = 11.2$), although controlling for age, gender, race, education, income, and current number of children, this difference was not significant ($F < 1$). There was no significant difference between the two samples with respect to number of surviving children ($t < 1.0$; Bereaved $M = 3.48$ vs. Control $M = 3.25$).

There was also no significant difference at either interview in the number of recent life events (excluding the loss of a child; main effect and Wave X Bereaved/Control interaction $Fs < 1$). Neither were bereaved more or less likely than controls to have experienced within three years of each interview any of the seven events making up the scale (Chi-squares $< 1.2, ps > .25$).

In summary, then, relative to controls, bereaved parents were more likely to be older, widowed, and women with less education and slightly less income. A greater proportion of these bereaved parents were African American who, including their deceased child, had a greater number of offspring. Both the bereaved and control participants had similar numbers of recent traumatic events of their lives, with the exception of the loss of a child, and there were no differences in the temporal distance from these events.

Bereaved versus Controls

Measures of Adjustment

All four measures of adjustment were moderately intercorrelated. Consistent across both waves, health and depression were most highly correlated (average $r = .50$), whereas relations of marital satisfaction to health were lowest across the two waves (average $r = .11$). To test for differences in adjustment between the bereaved and control groups, a series of four (one for each adjustment variable) 2 (Wave) × 2 (Bereaved/Control) repeated measures ANCOVAs were conducted. Demographic variables (age, gender, marital status, race, education, and income) were covaried in each analysis.[2] Analyses revealed a significant difference only on the depression measure, ($F(1,1056) = 5.56, p < .02$), with the bereaved reporting higher levels of depression. A marginal effect was also found for marital satisfaction ($F(1,599) = 3.06, p < .10$), such that the bereaved parents (who were in a marital relationship) reported slightly greater marital satisfaction. Controlling for age, gender, income, race, and number of children, those bereaved parents not in a marital relationship tended to be more depressed than those currently in a relationship ($F(1,1057) = 6.54, p = .01$).

In general, measures of adjustment were relatively stable across the two time points. Only one of the analyses suggested change over time. The ANCOVA

---

[2] For marital satisfaction, gender, race, education, age, and number of children were significant covariates; for CES-D, marital status, race, education, and income, were significant covariates; for self-esteem, education and income were significant covariates; and for health, education, income, and age were significant covariates.

for health indicated a significant decrease in perceived health from Wave 1 to Wave 2, as might be expected given the age of samples ($F(1,1073) = 22.65$, $p < .001$). This effect was qualified, however, by a significant Bereaved by Wave interaction ($F(1,1073) = 5.51$, $p < .02$). Simple effects analyses suggested that whereas the perceived health ratings of the two groups did not differ at Wave 1, the parentally-bereaved sample showed a greater decrement in health by Wave 2, suggesting that their health was deteriorating at a faster rate than for controls (even after controlling for the effects of age).

Sources of Satisfaction

When asked what were their greatest sources of satisfaction or pleasure, the parentally-bereaved respondents offered, on average, 2.16 sources of satisfaction per person. The control respondents offered, on average, 2.32 sources of satisfaction. After controlling for age, race, education, marital status, and gender of respondent, no differences in the number of sources of satisfaction were observed between bereaved and non-bereaved ($F = 1.04$, ns.). However, women offered a greater number of sources of satisfaction than did men (Beta = $.167, p < .001$).

Although bereaved and non-bereaved parents did not differ in the number of reported sources of satisfaction, there were notable differences in the *specific* sources of satisfaction the two groups identified, although these differences were limited to women. As Table 2 illustrates, parentally-bereaved women were less

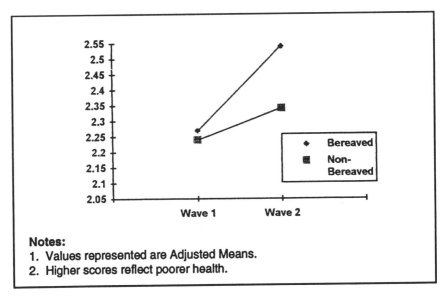

Notes:
1. Values represented are Adjusted Means.
2. Higher scores reflect poorer health.

Figure 1. Perceived health ratings of bereaved and non-bereaved parents over the two interview waves.

Table 2. Sources of Satisfaction and Pleasure Reported by Bereaved and Non-Bereaved Parents

Source of Satisfaction/Pleasure	Men (%)		Women (%)	
	Bereaved	Non-Ber.	Bereaved	Non-Ber.
Family	52.9	41.0	36.7	55.7**
Work	11.8	18.1	3.3	11.2#
Possessions/Assets	11.8	7.6	2.3	8.6
Health	11.8	6.7	5.0	7.0
Interpersonal/Social	23.5	18.9	26.7	32.6
Leisure	52.9	63.1	55.0	52.9
Church/Religion	5.9	9.6	30.0	20.5#
Other	0	5.8	10.0	7.2
Nothing/ No Source of Satisfaction	0	0.6	0	0.5
Mean Sources of Satisfaction	2.24	2.12	2.13	2.24
n	17	344	60	654

Notes: Percentages denote the proportion of respondents mentioning at least one source of satisfaction/pleasure from the category. Percentages add to more than 100 percent because respondents frequently offered more than one source of satisfaction.

Significance of Chi-squares ($df = 1$) for Bereaved parent vs. Non-bereaved parent for men and women is given by:
#$p < .15$
**$p < .01$

likely to mention family and work, and were more likely to mention religion, as sources of satisfaction relative to non-parentally bereaved women.

Sources of Problems or Worries

When asked what were their greatest sources of problems or worry, the parentally-bereaved respondents offered, on average, 1.57 sources of worry. The control respondents offered, on average, 1.50 sources of worry. After controlling for age, race, education, marital status, and gender of respondent, no differences in the number of sources of worry were observed between bereaved and non-bereaved ($F = 1.83, p > .15$). Significant effects with gender and age were noted (Gender: Beta = .188; Age: Beta = –.102, $ps < .002$). such that women provided more sources of worry than men, and younger respondents reported more worries than older respondents.

Although bereaved and non-bereaved parents did not differ in the reported number of worries, there was one difference in the specific worries reported by the two groups. As Table 3 shows, across both men and women, the parentally bereaved were more likely to report worrying about death.[3]

Within Bereaved Analyses

Of the four measures of adjustment obtained at Wave 1, the bereaved respondents' self-rating of how well they had dealt with the loss of their child (i.e., self-rated recovery, asked at Wave 1) was correlated significant only with depression ($r(75) = .36$, $p = .001$). Importantly, self-ratings of recovery were not significantly related to time since the death ($r = -.05$). Similarly, time since the death was not related significantly to depression ($r = .05$). Indeed, of the measures of adjustment, time since the loss was correlated significantly only with health, such that poorer perceived health was associated with greater time since the loss ($r = .28$, $p < .02$). The effects described above were not lessened significantly after statistically controlling for age, gender, education, race, and income.

Of the demographic variables, the most significant predictor of adjustment was the number of negative events that the bereaved had recently experienced. After controlling for age, gender, education, race, and income, greater number of recent negative events was associated with poorer perceived health ($r = .27$, $p < .05$). This association was also observed at Wave 2 ($r = .30$, $p = .01$).

Relations of Loss Characteristics to Adjustment and Recovery

In general, there were few significant differences in adjustment or recovery attributable to loss factors. There were two weak exceptions to this pattern, however. The loss of a daughter, as opposed to a son, was weakly associated with a perceived failure to recover ($t(75) = 1.74$, $p < .10$), but not with any of the other measures of adjustment ($ps > .25$). As well, surprisingly, perceived health was somewhat worse at both waves if the loss was expected than if it was unexpected ($F(1,73) = 8.49$, $p < .01$), although differences were not evident for the expected/unexpected factor on other adjustment variables.

DISCUSSION

This longitudinal study examined the long-term psychological and somatic aftermath of later life parental bereavement. Significant consequences were observed, although there was also much comparability between the bereaved and non-bereaved groups. In addition, the socio-demographic and personal context

---

[3] Of the five bereaved parents mentioning worrying about death, 3 worried about the death of their child, 2 worried about their own death. Of the 15 controls, 7 worried about the death of their spouse, 5 worried about their own death, 3 worried about the death of friends or relatives.

Table 3. Sources of Worry Reported by Bereaved and Non-Bereaved Parents

Source of Worry	Men (%)		Women (%)	
	Bereaved	Non-Ber.	Bereaved	Non-Ber.
Family	5.9	20.9	28.3	36.4
Work	5.9	9.3	0	5.7
Possessions/Assets/ Financial Security	23.5	27.0	25.0	27.4
Health	29.4	35.2	46.7	46.2
Death	11.8	2.3[#]	5.0	1.1*
Interpersonal/Social	0	0	1.7	0.8
Loss of Independence	5.9	2.3	10.0	5.2
Other	23.5	13.7	23.3	14.5[#]
Nothing/No Source of Worry	17.6	21.5	15.0	10.6
Mean Sources of Worry	1.35	1.27	1.63	1.62
n	17	344	60	654

Notes: Percentages denote the proportion of respondents mentioning at least one source of worry from the category. Percentages add to more than 100 percent because many respondents offered more than one source of worry.
Significance of Chi-squares ($df = 1$) for Bereaved parent vs. Non-bereaved parent for men and women is given by:
[#]$p < .15$
*$p < .05$

within which the bereavement took place emerged as important considerations. These consequences and context effects guide the discussion that follows, concluding with a brief evaluation of the study and comment on its implications.

Consequences of Later Life Parental Bereavement

The psychological consequences of later life parental bereavement uncovered in this study range from marked and direct to subtle and indirect in nature. For example, bereaved parents reported significantly greater depression, supporting both expectations and previous research [e.g., 26, 28]. Importantly, this was a depression over which time had apparently little effect, as depression levels and other measures of psychological adjustment were unrelated to time since loss, reminiscent of Florian's findings [32]. A notable exception to this pattern was perceived health which was identified as poorer with increased time since the death. Further evidence of this degenerative physical effect resides in the finding that health deteriorated significantly faster for the bereaved parents relative to controls over the two waves of the study and the mortality rate of the bereaved parents was slightly, although nonsignificantly, higher than that of controls (comparable to that reported in [34]). Taken together, these results may be seen as supportive of Gorer's observation that ". . . it may be literally true . . . that the parents never get over [their loss]" [22, p. 121] (see also [10]) and of Rando's [3] claim that parental grief appears to go unresolved. Birren [41] has suggested that later life parental bereavement is the functional equivalent of the addition of ten years onto an individual's chronological age; the above noted effects attest to the toll that such an addition takes.

The effects of later life parental bereavement were not uniformly negative, however. This is a point frequently misplaced in bereavement research with its primary focus on depression [see 42] to the exclusion of other outcomes, both positive *and* negative [see 7, 8]. The bereaved parents in this study who were currently married reported slightly, although non-significantly, *greater* marital satisfaction than the married, non-bereaved. In general, married individuals tended to report less depression. Later life marriage may serve as a source of emotional support for bereaved parents in contrast to younger parents [see 10], for whom marital dissolution is not an infrequent outcome. Later life, more generally, may also be associated with a greater comparability of emotional expression for women and men [e.g., 43], perhaps offering a framework for understanding the greater discrepancy in the experiences of younger and older bereaved fathers in contrast to comparably aged mothers [30].

Another example of outcomes in the general province of the positive, and of a more indirect nature, include the findings on sources of satisfaction. Recall that the bereaved and the non-bereaved did not differ in the number of sources from which satisfaction was derived (or in which worries were positioned). Parentally-bereaved women, however, were less likely to mention family and work and were more likely to mention religion as sources of satisfaction than were those women not bereft of an adult child. Additionally, bereaved parents were more likely to report worrying about death than the non-bereaved parents. Perhaps issues of attachment and self-identification underlie these sources of satisfaction and worry as bereaved parents struggle with who they are in a world made chaotic by their child's death. The uncovering of these effects would be lost in the more scalar approaches to bereavement and are suggestive of provocative differences in orientation and responses to life in bereavement.

Context Effects

The indirect nature of above-noted consequences is shared by the demographic differences and covariates effects which, in the aggregate, underscore the importance of attending to the socio-demographic context in which bereavement and adaptation occur [23]. As Averill and Nunley have identified, emotional reactions to bereavement cannot be isolated from other social phenomena and the course of time during which such reactions take place [44].

For example, it is of particular relevance that in the ten years preceding Wave 1 of this study, 5 percent of this random sample of American adults had lost a child (of any age) more than half of whom were parents at least fifty years of age. This does not represent a small and insignificant sample of the population and takes on heightened importance against a backdrop of population aging. Moss et al. have reminded us that a woman aged sixty-five or over has a one-in-four chance of outliving a son [11]! Furthermore, this sample is not normally distributed in the overall parent population: African Americans were significantly over-represented among bereaved parents. These racial differences in the prevalence of parental bereavement, and their psychosocial adaptation correlates, merit further investigation.

The bereaved sample, relative to controls, was also disproportionately female, older, less likely to be married, and more likely to be widowed. When these characteristics are combined with the finding that those currently not married were more depressed than those who were married, an image emerges of a context in which individuals are struggling with and suffering from the multiple social and interpersonal losses of their lives; perhaps this reflects what Kastenbaum has described as "bereavement overload" [36]. Preliminary support for this interpretation is offered by the finding that, at both waves of the study, those who reported a greater number of recent negative events also reported poorer health. This parallels the more dramatic findings of Levav et al. who reported higher mortality rates among spouseless bereaved parents [35].

Additional challenges to successful adaptation include the slightly lower income and the lower levels of education that bereaved parents report. Earlier research has suggested a positive association between education and adjustment for older bereaved parents [45]; in fact, Lopata [37] has concluded that the degree of education may be the most influential variable, providing the ability to clarify problems, to identify available resources, and to take action toward possible solutions [9].

The context of bereavement, however, involves more than the sociodemographic features by which populations might be characterized. As Stroebe et al. have suggested, understanding the aspects of life connected with the loss will offer avenues for the assessment of adaptation [42]. This includes some recognition of the personal and social meaning of the nature and quality of the relationship that has been lost. For example, similar to the findings of Shanfield and Swain [26], the loss of a daughter was modestly (although not significantly) associated with a sense of having dealt more poorly with the death and the concomitant problems. Perhaps this reflects the closer relationships that have been found to exist between parents (and especially mothers) and their daughters.

Perhaps, also, this bears upon issues of caregiver access, either real or anticipated, given the prevalence of women (including large numbers of adult daughters) fulfilling the duties and responsibilities of caregiver. Expected losses were associated with poorer perceived health than were unexpected losses perhaps in this instance attesting to the costs of caregiving and/or the fact that the parents themselves were older and perhaps more likely to decline. These remain hypotheses at this point in the absence of additional data.

Study Evaluation and Implications

The ACL survey provided an unique, although imperfect, opportunity to examine the long-term and ongoing effects of later life parental bereavement. Significant strengths of the ACL include its longitudinal nature (although this added surprisingly little to the results of this investigation), the representative sampling characteristics and the fact that the bereaved were not informed prior to the interview that they would be discussing the loss of their child. In addition, the inclusion of a large and appropriate comparison group and the controlling of various socio-demographic factors facilitated by the broad battery assessed in the ACL are improvements over previous research. For example, as previously identified, a major deficiency in this area of study has been the reliance on relatively small, homogeneous, and special bereavement groups (e.g., self-help groups) or clinical populations for study samples. The random sampling in the ACL minimized the "priming effects" inherent in such samples and sampling strategies which may at least partially account for the lack of differences between the two groups on several of the measures.

This, however, also raises one of the limitations of the approach taken in this study and, in general, the use of data not explicitly collected for the study of (parental) bereavement. For example, guilt, rumination, anger/hostility or even grief were not assessed in this study. Suggested here is that finer levels and more sensitive and/or pointed types of measurement may better uncover some of the complexities of parental bereavement. An example of this thinking may be found in the results concerning the sources of worry and satisfaction, perhaps more generally reflective of changes in orientation to life as a consequence of parental bereavement. Similarly, death and the complexities of bereavement happen to and within families and culture [9]; a more thorough knowledge of family dynamics and the cultural and/or racial customs in bereavement would add to our understanding of the personal, familial, and social meanings of what has been lost and a better appreciation of the many complex, profound and often subtle ways in which individuals grieve. As such, the results of this study should be seen as more evocative than definitive.

Implicit in the above are several overlapping implications of this study for subsequent theory, research, and practice. For example, this study questions the chronological, linear, and endpoint-oriented approach to bereavement suggesting instead a more long-term, complex and fluid understanding of the process [see also 46]. The exclusiveness of this process to parental bereavement has yet to be determined, although it has been advanced elsewhere [6]. Researchers are encouraged to move beyond the conventional temporal markers and indicators of adjustment in their assessment of bereavement trajectories. Attention should be drawn to the context within which bereavement takes place as informed by SES indicators, as well as race, gender, age, and life experiences (including other losses). For example, can there ever be an older non-bereft sample; is it reasonable to assume that the older non-bereaved of this study are not bereft of any significant individual of their lives [e.g., 47]? Reactions to death may best be understood in the context of other losses experienced by the bereft. Our attempt to explore this (i.e., the number of negative events, including widowhood) was inadequate given that we could not ascertain other losses such as the death of a friend or sibling. Similarly, as suggested by de Vries and others [e.g., 9, 13] as well as some of the within-bereaved analyses reported here, family dynamics play a role not limited to the gender of the deceased child and circumstances of the death; future research might consider exploring the effects of birth order, only children, only sons or daughters, or prior relationship evaluation (e.g., favored child, child "most likely to succeed"). The fluidity and complexity suggested by the above serve as important reminders for what many clinicians already know and practice: the courses and consequences of bereavement assume many forms and the failure to follow some prescribed and normative recovery patterns need not be interpreted as a coping failure [e.g., 48].

CONCLUSION

This study provides evidence of both significant difference and substantial consistency between a group of older bereaved parents and a comparison population. The differences and interpreted consequences of parent bereavement are articulated above; recall as well that bereaved parents did not differ from controls on a number of measures including self-esteem or perceived health (at Wave 1). Several of the findings were of only marginal statistical significance (e.g., marital satisfaction). The patterns of change over the two waves of the study were largely comparable for the groups. Perhaps a conclusion to draw, as suggested by other researchers, is that older bereaved adults demonstrate significant hardiness and resilience [e.g., 49, 50] or even, perhaps, indifference. Alternatively, it may be that those suffering the most may become institutionalized or may themselves succumb. The foregoing account attests to the complexity of the bereavement process, the context within which it takes place, and the sometimes subtle positive and negative changes that take place over extended periods of time.

REFERENCES

1. F. H. Brown, The Impact of Death and Serious Illness on the Family Life Cycle, in *The Changing Family Life Cycle: A Framework for Family Therapy* (2nd Edition), E. Carter and M. McGoldrick (eds.), Allyn & Bacon, Boston, pp. 457-481, 1989.
2. C. M. Sanders, A Comparison of Adult Bereavement in the Death of a Spouse, Child and Parent, *Omega: Journal of Death and Dying, 10*:4, pp. 303-322, 1979-80.
3. T. A. Rando, Parental Bereavement: An Exception to the General Conceptualizations of Mourning, in *Parental Loss of a Child*, T. A. Rando (ed.), Research Press, Champaign, Illinois, pp. 45-40, 1986.
4. S. S. Rubin, The Death of a Child is Forever: The Life Course Impact of Child Loss, in *Handbook of Bereavement: Theory, Research and Intervention*, M. S. Stroebe, W. Stroebe, and R. O. Hansson (eds.), Cambridge University Press, New York, pp. 285-299, 1993.
5. M. Osterweis, F. Solomon, and M. Green, *Bereavement: Reactions, Consequences and Care*, National Academy Press, Washington, D.C., 1984.
6. D. Klass and S. J. Marwit, Toward a Model of Parental Grief, *Omega: Journal of Death and Dying, 19*:1, pp. 31-50, 1988-89.
7. C. B. Wortman and R. C. Silver, Coping with Irrevocable Loss, in *Cataclysms, Crises and Catastrophes, Psychology in Action*, G. R. VandenBos and B. K. Bryant (eds.), American Psychological Association, Washington, D.C., pp. 189-235, 1987.
8. C. B. Wortman and R. C. Silver, The Myths of Coping with Loss, *Journal of Consulting and Clinical Psychology, 57*:3, pp. 349-357, 1989.
9. N. W. Arbuckle and B. de Vries, The Long-Term Effects of Later Life Spousal and Parental Bereavement on Personal Functioning, *Gerontologist, 5*, pp. 637-647, 1995.
10. D. R. Lehman, C. B. Wortman, and A. Williams, Long-Term Effects of Losing a Spouse or Child in a Motor Vehicle Crash, *Journal of Personality and Social Psychology, 52*:1, pp. 218-231, 1987.
11. M. S. Moss, E. L. Lesher, and S. Z. Moss, Impact of the Death of an Adult Child on Elderly Parents: Some Observations, *Omega: Journal of Death and Dying, 17*:3, pp. 209-218, 1986-87.
12. B. Raphael, *The Anatomy of Bereavement*, Basic Books, New York, 1983.
13. B. de Vries, R. Dalla Lana, and V. T. Falck, Parental Bereavement over the Life Course: A Theoretical Intersection and Empirical Review, *Omega: Journal of Death and Dying, 29*:1, pp. 47-69, 1994.
14. I. D. Yalom, *Love's Executioner and Other Tales of Psychotherapy*, Basic Books, New York, 1989.
15. T. Benedek, The Family as a Psychologic Field, in *Parenthood: Its Psychology and Psychopathology*, E. J. Anthony and T. Benedek (eds.), Little, Brown and Company, London, pp. 109-136, 1970.
16. M. McGoldrick and F. Walsh, A Time to Mourn: Death and the Family Life Cycle, in *Living Beyond the Loss: Death in the Family*, F. Walsh and M. McGoldrick (eds.), W. W. Norton & Company, New York, pp. 30-49, 1991.
17. P. B. Baltes, H. W. Reese, and L. P. Lipsitt, Life-Span Developmental Psychology, *Annual Review of Psychology, 31*, pp. 65-110, 1980.

18. R. Kastenbaum, Dying and Death: A Life-Span Approach, in *Handbook of the Psychology of Aging* (2nd Edition), J. E. Birren and K. W. Schaie (eds.), Van Nostrand Reinhold, New York, pp. 619-643, 1985.
19. H. W. Perkins and L. B. Harris, Familial Bereavement and Health in Adult Life Course Perspective, *Journal of Marriage and the Family, 52*, pp. 337-356, 1990.
20. P. C. Rosenblatt, *Bitter, Bitter Tears: Nineteenth Century Diarists and Twentieth-Century Grief Theories*, University of Minnesota Press, Minneapolis, Minnesota, 1983.
21. M. A. Lieberman, All Family Losses are Not Equal, *Journal of Family Psychology, 2*:3, pp. 368-372, 1989.
22. G. Gorer, *Death, Grief and Mourning*, Doubleday, Garden City, New York, 1965.
23. M. S. Stroebe, R. O. Hansson, and W. Stroebe, Contemporary Themes and Controversies in Bereavement Research, in *Handbook of Bereavement: Theory, Research, and Intervention*, M. S. Stroebe, W. Stroebe, and R. O. Hansson (eds.), Cambridge University Press, New York, pp. 457-475, 1993.
24. R. Weiss, Loss and Recovery, in *Handbook of Bereavement: Theory, Research and Intervention*, M. S. Stroebe, W. Stroebe, and R. O. Hansson (eds.), Cambridge University Press, New York, pp. 271-284, 1993.
25. S. Freud, Mourning and Melancholia, in *The Standard Edition of the Complete Original Works of Sigmund Freud, 14*, J. Strachey (ed. and trans.), Hogarth Press, London, United Kingdom, pp. 152-170, 1957. (Original work published in 1917.)
26. B. Shanfield and B. J. Swain, Death of Adult Children in Traffic Accidents, *Journal of Nervous and Mental Disease, 172*:9, pp. 533-538, 1984.
27. L. Videka-Sherman and M. A. Lieberman, The Effects of Self-Help and Psychotherapy Intervention on Child Loss: The Limits of Recovery, *American Journal of Orthopsychiatry, 55*:1, pp. 70-82, 1985.
28. E. L. Lesher and K. J. Bergey, Bereaved Elderly Mothers: Changes in Health, Functional Activities, Family Cohesion and Psychological Well-Being, *International Journal of Aging and Human Development, 26*:2, pp. 81-90, 1988.
29. S. S. Rubin, Death of the Future?: An Outcome Study of Bereaved Parents in Israel, *Omega: Journal of Death and Dying, 20*:4, pp. 323-339, 1989-90.
30. W. C. Fish, Differences of Grief Intensity in Bereaved Parents, in *Parental Loss of a Child*, T. A. Rando (ed.), Research Press, Champaign, Illinois, pp. 415-430, 1986.
31. S. S. Rubin, Adult Child Loss and the Two-Track Model of Bereavement, *Omega: Journal of Death and Dying, 24*:3, pp. 183-202, 1991-92.
32. V. Florian, Meaning and Purpose of Life of Bereaved Parents whose Son Fell during Active Military Service, *Omega: Journal of Death and Dying, 20*:2, pp. 91-102, 1989-90.
33. B. Shanfield, G. A. Benjamin, and B. J. Swain, Parents' Response to the Death of Adult Children from Accidents and Cancer: A Comparison. *Omega: Journal of Death and Dying, 17*, pp. 289-297, 1986-87.
34. I. Levav, Mortality and Psychopathology following the Death of an Adult Child: An Epidemiological Review, *Israel Journal of Psychiatry Related Sciences, 19*:1, pp. 23-28, 1982.
35. I. Levav, Y. Friedlander, J. Kark, and E. Peritz, An Epidemiologic Study of Mortality among Bereaved Parents, *New England Journal of Medicine, 319*, pp. 457-461, 1988.
36. R. Kastenbaum, Death and Bereavement in Later Life, in *Death and Bereavement*, A. H. Kutscher (ed.), Charles C. Thomas, Springfield, Illinois, pp. 28-54, 1969.

37. H. Z. Lopata, The Support Systems of American Urban Widows, in *Handbook of Bereavement: Theory, Research and Intervention*, M. S. Stroebe, W. Stroebe, and R. O. Hansson (eds.), Cambridge University Press, New York, pp. 381-396, 1993.
38. J. S. House, *Americans' Changing Lives: Wave 1, Computer File, 1986*; Producer, Survey Research Center, Ann Arbor, Michigan, 1989; Distributor, Inter-University Consortium for Political and Social Research, Ann Arbor, Michigan, 1990.
39. L. S. Radloff, The CES-D Scale: A Self-Report Depression Scale for Research in the General Population, *Applied Psychological Measurement, 1*:3, pp. 384-401, 1977.
40. M. Rosenberg, *Society and the Adolescent Self-Image*, Princeton University Press, Princeton, New Jersey, 1965.
41. J. E. Birren, personal communication, 1989.
42. M. S. Stroebe, W. Stroebe, and R. O. Hansson, Bereavement Research: An Historical Introduction, *Journal of Social Issues, 44*:3, pp. 1-18, 1988.
43. R. W. Levenson, L. I. Carstensen, W. V. Friesen, and P. Ekman, Emotion, Physiology, and Expression in Old Age, *Psychology and Aging, 6*, pp. 28-35, 1991.
44. J. R. Averill and E. P. Nunley, Grief as an Emotion and as a Disease: A Social-Constructionist Perspective, in *Handbook of Bereavement: Theory, Research and Intervention*, M. S. Stroebe, R. Hansson, and W. Stroebe (eds.), Cambridge University Press, New York, pp. 77-90, 1993.
45. R. Purisman, and B. Maoz, Adjustment and War Bereavement—Some Considerations, *British Journal of Medical Psychology, 50*, pp. 1-9, 1977.
46. D. A. Lund, Conclusions about Bereavement in Later Life and Implications for Interventions and Future Research, in *Older Bereaved Spouses: Research with Practical Applications*, D. A. Lund (ed.), Hemisphere, New York, pp. 215-231, 1989.
47. B. de Vries, A. J. Lehman, and N. Arbuckle, *Reactions to the Death of a Close Friend in Later Life*, paper presented at the annual meeting of the Gerontological Society of America, Los Angeles, November 1995.
48. D. R. Lehman, B. de Vries, C. B. Wortman, M. Haring, and R. G. Tweed, *Recovery from the Perspective of the Bereaved: Personal Assessments and Sources of Distress and Support*, unpublished manuscript, University of British Columbia, 1996.
49. M. S. Caserta and D. Lund, Bereavement Stress and Coping among Older Adults: Expectations versus the Actual Experience, *Omega: Journal of Death and Dying, 25*:1, pp. 33-45, 1992.
50. R. R. McCrae and P. R. Costa, Psychological Resilience among Widowed Men and Women: A 10-Year Follow-Up of a National Sample, *Journal of Social Issues, 44*:3, pp. 129-142, 1988.

GRANDPARENTS' REACTIONS TO THE DEATH OF A GRANDCHILD: AN EXPLORATORY FACTOR ANALYTIC STUDY*

P. S. FRY, PH.D.
Trinity Western University, Canada

ABSTRACT

One hundred and fifty-two grandparents who had experienced the death of a grandchild in the preceding three years or so served as subjects for two separate but related studies investigating the multidimensional nature of the grief reactions of grandparents. In Study 1, subjects responded to an open-ended questionnaire which asked for brief descriptions of their grief reactions immediately following the death of the grandchild, and perceived changes in their affective and behavioral responses with the passage of time. A principal component factor analysis procedure was used to identify the major dimensions in the grief reactions of grandparents. Of the six factors that emerged, Factor 1 (Emotional Rupturing) and Factor 2 (Survivor Guilt) accounted for 21.0 percent and 18.6 percent, respectively, of the total variance. In Study 2, a six-month longitudinal follow-up of seventeen grandparents was conducted by means of in-depth interviews. Subjects provided detailed personal accounts of their coping and recovery processes. Interview data were analyzed using a qualitative approach. The results of Study 2 corroborated and supported the factor analysis results obtained in Study 1. Both studies highlight the continuing need for gerontologists to investigate the complexity of grandparents' grief reactions. The studies draw attention to the mental health implications for older adults who have experienced loss and bereavement.

---

*This study was supported, in part, by a research grant from the Social Sciences and Humanities Research Council of Canada (Strategic Grants, File #492-87-0006) awarded to the author while on Faculty at the University of Calgary, Alberta.

© 1997, Baywood Publishing Co., Inc.

Previous research on the grief and bereavement of grandparents is very limited. Nevertheless, there is sufficient evidence [e.g., 1-5] pointing to the complexity of the grief that grandparents experience over the loss of a grandchild. Wedemeyer notes that grief is likely to be experienced with varying degrees of intensity and wide diversity depending, of course, on the nature of involvement with the deceased person, and nature of the relationship with the family before the tragic event [6]. Link [7] observes that due to the increase in life-spans more grandparents are participating in the grandparent role for longer periods of time, and also with increasing levels of responsibility for care taking and child-rearing occurring among young grandparents [8-11]. Since grandparents continue to be parents for an increasing period of time [7], many of the interactions with their children provide a unique context in which a complex bonding and attachment relationship may develop with the grandchildren [3, 7, 12]. Therefore, it seems reasonable to assume that the impact of the death of a grandchild would be particularly difficult, powerful and pervasive because of the unique role that increasing numbers of grandparents, both younger and older, have in the family system [7, 9-11]. Given that grandparents expect to predecease their grandchildren even more than parents expect to predecease their children, it is to be expected that most grandparents would experience feelings of sadness, loss, sorrow, and emptiness equal in intensity to similar feelings experienced by the parents of the deceased child [4]. Commenting on the complexity of grandparents' grief reactions, Ponzetti observes that when a grandchild dies the grandparents' grief is three-fold: They grieve for the deceased grandchild, their son or daughter who parented the child, and they grieve for themselves as individuals [4, 5]. There is also the additional anxiety that as elders they will become the forgotten grievers in the family bereavement [5, 13, 14]. Lately, researchers are beginning to recognize the grave implications which the grandparents' loss of a relationship with the grandchild has for the mental health of elders [3, 8, 9]. There is also growing recognition of the fact that to overlook the grandparents' grief reactions is to ignore a vital element of the process of bereavement of elderly persons [15, 16] and its pervasive effect on the long term mental health of older individuals [14]. To date, however, there has been very limited research done to investigate the intensity or diversity of grandparents' grief reactions.

The purpose of the present study, therefore, was to conduct an exploratory but systematic examination of the various dimensions of the grief process of the grandparents over the loss of a grandchild, and to obtain a somewhat clearer picture of the perceptions and images they project on the loss. Although the literature presents a few observations about the grief of grandparents based on clinical experiences and theory, there is a need for systematic research to empirically describe the major underlying themes of grandparents' grief. Our conceptualization for this study is predicated on the notion that data are needed to explore the themes of the untimeliness of the death of the young person, the uniqueness of the grandparent-child bond, and the impact of the loss on the present and long-term psychological functioning of the grandparents [17-19]. The search for such normative information is important to family members, and also to service providers who must provide bereavement support to grandparents as important members of the extended family [15, 16, 20].

The present investigation was conducted in two separate but related studies (Study 1 and Study 2). Study 1 was aimed at obtaining quantitative data concerning major themes underlying the immediate and long-term grief reactions of the grandparents to the death of the grandchild. Study 2 was concerned with obtaining qualitative data through in-depth interviews, and following up on "leads" about generic themes of grief and bereavement which emerged from the quantitative data.

STUDY 1

Following leads provided by previous researchers [5, 17, 19, 20] concerning the strong psychological impact that "off-time" tragic events may have on elderly grandparents' and their ability to withstand the grief they have sustained, the purpose of Study 1 was to explore the multidimensionality of the grandparents' bereavement and to identify the beliefs, fears, and anxieties associated with the death of the grandchild.

Method

Sample

A convenience sample of 152 grandparents who had experienced the death of a grandchild was located through a "call for volunteers" notice that was posted in the social waiting rooms and lounges of senior citizens' centers and seniors' housing complexes, and in the newsletters of some of the seniors' centers, in Southern Alberta (e.g., Calgary, Airdrie, Cochrane, Crossfield, High River, Lethbridge, and Red Deer). The single most important criterion which all volunteer individuals had to meet was the experience of the death of a grandchild through natural causes, accident, or suicide in the previous three years or less.

One hundred and seventy-eight individuals who met the criterion and responded to the call for volunteers were contacted by telephone and were informed that the purpose of the study was to investigate the grief reactions of the grandparents. The volunteers were told that they would receive, through the mail, a questionnaire that would ask them to write about their thoughts, feelings, reactions, and recollections concerning the death of the grandchild. Of the 178 volunteers who were contacted, twenty-six declined the invitation to participate because of their personal disability of difficulty in reading, or in writing their responses to the questionnaire. The questionnaire designed for the study was mailed to the remaining 152 individuals who volunteered their participation in the study.

All participants were assured about anonymity and confidentiality of information they provided. They were assured that all questionnaire response materials would be destroyed as soon as the data were coded, and definitely within four months of their returning the questionnaire to us. Thirty-eight individuals telephoned research assistants to ask for additional help in responding to the questionnaire. Fifteen individuals' responses were incomplete on one section of the questionnaire but their remaining responses were sufficiently detailed so as to be coded.

Participants recruited for the study were forty-five men and 107 women. Their ages ranged from fifty-two to eighty-two years and the mean age was 66.19 (SD = 5.92) for women, and 64.32 (SD = 8.61) for men. Later analysis of the participant pool composition revealed that there were sixteen husband-wife couples that responded to the questionnaire. The respondents reported an average of 3.2 children (range = 1 to 5), and an average of 3.8 living grandchildren (range = 1 to 11). Sixty-five percent of the 152 grandparents who were participants for this study were widowed. Fifty-two percent had at least a grade nine education, 25 percent reported having a baccalaureate degree, and the remaining 25 percent had a grade twelve education and some college courses. The majority (76%) affiliated with a protestant denomination.

Later analysis of the participant pool composition revealed that of the 152 participants recruited for the study, thirty-seven participants had experienced the death of a grandchild in six months or less preceding the time of the study. Seventy-seven participants reported losing a grandchild in the previous fourteen to eighteen months, and the remaining thirty-eight grandparents reported that death of the grandchild had occurred in the last thirty-two months preceding the time of the study.

A detailed analysis of the composition of the deceased grandchildren further revealed that their ages ranged from six years to thirty-two years. Of the deceased grandchildren, thirty-six (16 boys and 20 girls) were under the age of ten at the time of death. Another eighty grandchildren (67 boys and 13 girls) were between the ages of eleven and eighteen at the time of death. The remaining thirty-six deceased grandchildren (22 girls and 14 boys) were adults (25 years and over) at the time of death.

Development of the Questionnaire

Given the lack of empirical evidence from which to generate specific questions concerning the grief reactions of grandparents at the loss of a grandchild, the help of a focus group was solicited to develop some open-ended questions for the questionnaire to be mailed to the respondents. The use of a focus group is a widely accepted technique for the development of questionnaire items. The principal researcher and two graduate assistants had an in-depth interview and dialogue with a five-member focus group consisting of three grandparents (2 females, 1 male) who had experienced the loss of a grandchild in the past two years or more, one protestant chaplain who worked in a hospital setting, and one mother who had suffered the loss of a child. After much deliberation, the decision was made to use a completely open-ended format in order to elicit as much information as possible about the grandparents' reaction to the death, and also to allow the respondents to provide a personal narrative of the various parameters of their grief.

In Section 1 of the questionnaire, the respondents were encouraged to describe their physical symptoms, and their concerns, anxieties, or fears (both for themselves and for other members, separately) directly after they received the news about the grandchild's death.

In Section 2 of the questionnaire, the respondents were asked to describe the feelings they had a few months after the loss, and about their continuing concerns or anxieties both for themselves and other family members, as related to the death of the grandchild.

In Section 3 of the questionnaire, respondents were asked to describe their special bond, if any, with the grandchild and to write about noticeable changes they felt in their grief, and in their handling of the grief with the passage of time. Respondents were also asked to describe further the things they did, or what thoughts or activities, if any, assisted them to recover from the grief of losing a grandchild.

Finally, Section 4 of the questionnaire requested socio-demographic information, and more specific information concerning the cause of death, time, date, and year of the grandchild's death.

Blank space was provided at the end of each section, and respondents were encouraged to describe their feelings, concerns, or anxieties in their own words. They were also encouraged to add additional sheets of paper if they needed it for their responses. It should be noted that only eight of the 152 respondents used additional pages. Participants for Study 1 were recruited and data for the study were collected over a period of thirty days.

Coders

Coders were four senior undergraduate students who received a fifteen-hour training program for coding the participants' responses to specific questions into broad categories, in eliminating redundancies, and developing clusters of responses for purposes of data reduction. The responses of six confederate participants were used as the basis of a pilot training program organized for pairs of coders. Each coder was instructed to read a respondent's spontaneous responses to the three sections of the questionnaire, line by line. The structural unit of analysis, for coding purposes, was defined as a written communication of two to four lines. The individual coder was instructed to compile a master list of generic content themes that emerged from the responses (e.g., distress (stress), rejection, guilt, fear, anxiety, need for safety, protection, love and intimacy, desire to cry, run, escape, scream, or other similar feelings, thoughts, cognitions, and behavioral responses). Initially, coders-in-training compiled masters lists that included approximately sixty to eighty content items. Subsequently, coders were trained to re-evaluate the thematic contents of these items with a view to eliminating redundancies and avoiding overlappings among the content items. Coders, working in pairs, were instructed to synthesize the content items under twelve broad categories (4 categories for each of the 3 sections of the questionnaire). After this reduction to twelve categories was achieved, coders, working in pairs, were further trained to group and integrate the responses to fit into broad clusters of responses, for example, 1) *clusters of behavioral reactions* (e.g., crying, pacing, sobbing, shivering, shouting, choking); 2) *clusters of underlying emotions* (e.g., stress, guilt, sadness, depression, remorse, pain, and hurt); 3) *clusters of underlying beliefs, values and needs* (e.g., important to respect others' needs, important to protect/shield, important to support, important to avoid confrontation; need to give or receive physical affection); and 4) *clusters of underlying fears and anxieties* (e.g., fear of other persons' dying, anxiety about being forgotten, fear of isolation and loneliness, fear of the future).

In the final stages of training, coders were helped to develop numerical codes for specific content items, and to incorporate these code numbers with alphabetical codes for the twelve broad categories of responses and four clusters of responses. Training continued until pairs of coders reached a minimum of 85 percent agreement (range = 72 to 97%) in grouping responses across all characteristics considered.

Results

Factor Analyses of Grandparents' Reactions to the Loss of the Grandchild

Two steps were taken before performing the factor analyses. First, a panel of three professionals (social worker, bereavement therapist, developmental psychology professor) reviewed all of the twelve broad categories of responses into which the data had been coded by the student assistants. These categories were used by coders to extract statements that reflected recurrent themes of grief as amplified in the participants' responses to the first three sections of the questionnaire. The professionals rated the importance of maintaining each broad category along a 3-point scale of "not important, important, very important." This procedure yielded a total of nine overall categories that were rated as "important to very important" and a total of fifty-two items that were coded in these categories. In the second step, the number of items to be subjected to the exploratory factor analyses was reduced after examining each of the fifty-two items' measure of sampling adequacy (MSA). This measure indicates how well a variable's correlation with other variables in an instrument can be accounted for based on linear combinations of other variables [21]. Variables with an MSA coefficient of less than .7 were excluded because they showed little communality with other clustered variables in the questionnaire. The application of this factor analysis procedure [21, 22] resulted in a further reduction of the total number of items for use in the factor analysis. In the final analysis, thirty-two items were subjected to a principal component factor analysis. Items included in a factor were required to have factor loadings exceeding .5 on the primary factor, with the next highest factor loading differing by at least .2 (see factor loadings in Table 1). This detailed inspection revealed that participants' factors seemed to fall under six common categories of grandparents' grief responses and their concerns, anxieties, and regrets. Cattell's scree test and an analysis of the percentage of the total variance accounted for by the factors were performed in the factor analysis [23]. These categories, as well as the twenty-five items that made up the rotated factors, and the frequencies and factor loadings they yielded, are listed in Table 1. Table 1 shows that the major grief reactions of grandparents was composed of factors 1, 2, 3, 4, 5 and 6 derived from participants' responses to the three sections of the questionnaire.

Of the six factors identified, Factor 1 (Emotional Rupturing) and Factor 2 (Survivor Guilt) accounted for 21.0 percent and 18.6 percent, respectively, of the total variance. Factor 3 (Regrets About Relationship With Deceased Child) and Factor 4 (Need to Restructure Relationship With Family Members and Living Grandchildren) accounted for another 10.5 percent and 9.2 percent, respectively, of the total variance. Finally, Factor 5 (Concomitant Anxieties) and Factor 6 (Recovery Process) accounted for 5.1 percent and 4.9 percent, respectively, of the total variance.

DISCUSSION

The study identified several key factors highlighting commonalities in grandparents' grief reactions. The findings draw attention to the multidimensional nature of the grief which grandparents experience, and are suggestive of the mental health implications for bereaved older adults.

STUDY 2

The purpose of Study 2 was to better understand the complex nature of the grief and the emotional complications of bereavement in older adults as revealed in Study 1. The investigation was designed to include a six-month longitudinal follow-up of twelve grandmothers and five grandfathers who had recently lost a grandchild, less than six months ago, at the time that the study was initiated. The purpose of the longitudinal follow-up was to develop an in-depth understanding of the recovery process of grandparents after the loss of a grandchild. Using a

Table 1. Factor Analysis of Subjects' Response Reactions to Death of Grandchild

Subjects' Responses	Factor Loadings	Frequencies
Factor 1: Emotional Rupturing		
Feelings of disbelief, numbness, and shock	.655	112
Restlessness, confusion, and agitation	.591	94
Strong need to talk with deceased child's parents	.477	79
Sense of suffocating and claustrophobia	.346	72
Factor 2: Survivor Guilt		
Struggling with the notion that God is punishing me for past sins	.572	94
Struggling with feelings of self-doubt and guilt for being alive or needing to eat, sleep, etc.	.416	78
Struggling with the notion that it was my turn to die, not the grandchild's	.410	76
Need to apologize frequently to one's family for causing them grief	.347	69
Factor 3: Regrets about Relationship with Deceased Child		
Not telling the grandchild how much I loved him/her	.581	93
Not appreciating enough the grandchild's special qualities	.561	89
Concern about having disciplined the grandchild too frequently	.461	79
Concern that no one prepared the grandchild for dying and anxiety regarding death	.381	67
Factor 4: Need to Restructure Relationship with Family Members and Living Grandchildren		
Need to spend more time with family members	.561	92
Need to touch and hold living grandchildren	.418	76
Need to give grandchildren or foster grandchildren special gifts	.411	75
Need to share with family and children one's personal sense of survivor guilt	.477	79
Need to reassure family members and grandchildren that the deceased grandchild is safe and well	.397	69
Striving to be more tolerant and accepting of all children in general	.311	59

Table 1. (Cont'd.)

Subjects' Responses	Factor Loadings	Frequencies
Factor 5: Concomitant Anxieties		
Anxiety about losing other family members, including surviving grandchildren	.561	89
Anxiety about being too possessive of surviving grandchildren and their parents	.401	74
Anxiety about needing support vs. giving support to grandchildren and their parents	.321	61
Factor 6: Recovery Process		
Gradual re-engagement with non-family friends and social networks	.532	84
Gradual absorption in outside activities, including pursuit of work, fulfilling outside responsibilities and obligations	.482	83
Gradual absorption in routine activities	.377	67
Gradual absorption in working out "personal meaning for life" and searching for spiritual strength	.301	54

qualitative approach, a one and one-half hour semi-structured interview, which was audiotaped, was conducted with each grandparent, both initially, and approximately six months later. Participants were assured that the audiotapes and typescripts would be destroyed as soon as the data were transcribed. Assurance of confidentiality and anonymity of information was also given individually to each participant just prior to each interview. Formal permission to audiotape the interview was sought prior to each interview. Each grandparent described the meaning of their loss and their struggles to cope with the loss of the young life. A number of recurrent themes that emerged from the dialogues with grandparents corresponded pretty closely to the factors that were identified in the factor analyses results in Study 1.

Emotional Rupturing

Grandparents spoke of experiencing their grandchild's death as a sudden impact.

> All of a sudden this thing hits you. You feel like a part of you has been not just lost, but torn out of you and jabbed out of you. (Elsie)

Almost all grandmothers felt as though their whole world had been shattered.

> I feel it is not only Ronnie (grandson) who has been taken away, but also my daughter, and her children who have been taken away suddenly. Just everything is gone topsy turvy. I am afraid to talk with the children for fear that I will say the wrong thing or put my own pain before my daughter's. After all, my first thoughts should be for my daughter's pain. Suddenly all the joy has gone out of our lives and we don't talk anymore. Grandpa sits around. You can tell he is suffering, which is how I feel too . . . the grandchildren stay away as if they are afraid to upset us. Grandpa keeps reading his paper and doing the things he's used to doing. He doesn't feel like talking much with me, and he won't talk much with his daughter, either, when I put the phone in his hand. The only thing that helps me to feel better is by talking with my daughter about Ronnie and comforting her. It helps us both. (Alma, aged 65)

> I couldn't believe . . . that it actually happened . . . that I had seen Jessie (granddaughter) a month ago, and now she was gone. That was it. It was such an awful feeling, like someone plunging a knife into you. (Edna)

> It wasn't even real . . . It reminded me of a movie I had seen as a young girl; and I kept saying to myself, shouting it out, phone Hilda and Norton (they're my children) and they'll tell me it's a bad dream . . . but it wasn't a bad dream because Tom (my husband) sat me down, and said over and over again . . . he's gone, Amy, he's gone . . . you have to be strong for Hilda's sake. She'll need our support, Amy; but I kept saying: I still can't believe it . . . He is going to be back . . . (Amy, aged 59 years)

Shattered Belief Systems

The shattering of one's sense of groundedness in the world was echoed frequently in the words of several of the grandmothers. Several grandparents spoke about the shattering of a set of fundamental beliefs about the life of young ones that had previously guided their behavior and provided them with a sense of order and predictability in their lives. Many grandparents spoke about the grave untimeliness of the grandchild's death.

Wilma, who was quite frail and elderly and expected to die soon reflected her sorrow about the *"unfairness of life"* (see italics) for the sake of her own son whose child had died. Wilma's reminiscence also reflects much *"survivor guilt."*

> Your grandchild dying is worse than any death I've experienced before. Even when my husband died I was more ready for it, 'cause you know he was old, and I was sorry he went before me, but I accepted that he was supposed to go first, 'cause he was older. But you look at a healthy young person, and you say "that's not fair." *Fair would be if I could have died, 'cause I am old. I've had my life, but he was so young, you know, wasn't supposed to go before his*

grandparents and parents. I feel he had his whole future before him. His parents and we had so many hopes for him, we even joked with him about how he could look after us . . . and now he's gone. There's no way I can make the hurt any better for his parents because it is too major a tragedy, for them. *It just isn't fair that a young life was taken unexpectedly and here I am, useless and wasting, and allowed to live.*

I wish, somehow, I could take their pain away, my children's pain. I feel somehow I can handle my own pain 'cause I've been there before. My son is young, and for him his son's death is worse because there is no way out for him for a long time. I can handle the pain, 'cause I remind myself that I only have a few more years to live. *It's not fair that my son is only 40 and our grandson was only 13, and I worry that my son is so distressed that he'll neglect his other children. It's not fair to the other children either.* (Wilma, aged 81 years)

Grandparents' Feeling of Deep Sadness, Hurt, and Pain for the Adult Child

Grandmothers universally spoke of an inward type of movement in which they connected with their feelings of loss and grief. The following reminiscences reflect the complex nature of grandmothers' grief because of the sheer inability to separate it from the grief they feel for their children (see italics).

It wasn't until after Christmas and her first birthday was over that *I could really let it be, let it be—not just for myself, but for my daughter, also, who was not willing to let it go.*

I just walk around, and I feel sad every time I am with Martha (daughter). I know how deeply sad Martha feels. I feel very sad and lonely for Sarah too, and very hurt for Martha. *The pain of missing my grandchild, Sarah, and the pain of not being able to comfort Martha, my daughter, just eats away at me. If only I could say or do anything that would ease the pain my daughter feels. I can't make the pain any better for my daughter and I am afraid to talk about my grief with Martha because it would only make it more awful for her, right?* (Freda, aged 61)

It is hard to believe, but I feel my own sadness, and *then it hurts even more 'cause I feel sad for Gina, my daughter, and it hurts all over again, and more. I wish I could take away Gina's pain, but I know I can't.* She will have to let go of it herself. But I feel responsible as her mother to help her with her pain. All our children are special to us, but *I guess I feel a deep hurt for Gina right now. A day doesn't go by that I don't wish that I could make this thing better for Gina. My pain will go away, I know, but it's ten times more awful when I think of Gina's pain. If I could make the hurt and pain better for Gina, I think my own sadness would go away.* (Sharon, aged 69 years)

When Josh died, I felt like I had to touch base with my son, Rick, many times a day. It was like I had to just hear his voice that he was going to be okay. I knew nothing was going to happen to him, but then I had never thought anything would happen to Josh, either. If you think of it, Rick and Josh were together when Josh was knocked over, and there was nothing Rick could do; *but now I keep thinking that nothing, no, nothing must ever happen to Rick and I keep thinking about Rick's pain and Rick's troubles and what we can do to help him. It is almost as if we don't mind forgetting little Josh so it gives us more time to help Rick and his wife.* (Dorothy, aged 72 years)

Survivor Guilt

Grandparents do not infrequently search their lives to understand why the young one died and what they could do to ease their children's pain. Many feel a sense of guilt for living on and being an additional burden to their own children who must help them through the grief (see italics).

Total emptiness is what I feel. I look at myself in the mirror and I look at David's picture on the table, and I say "why him, why was he taken away?" Here I am . . . I get up in the morning, I eat, take a nap, and there's not much to do except to think. *Why couldn't it have been me in the coffin? If I had died in place of David, it would have been all right.* I've lived my life and have no more desires, but he (David) had so many things to live for, he had so many dreams and hopes; and his parents had hopes for his whole future. *I wish for my son's sake that David could have been spared and I could have died instead. It would have made so much more sense* . . . but this kind of thinking doesn't help you, it only makes the pain worse. (Albert, aged 82)

I often stop and think of my life and worry about the things I could have done to make it easier for our children. I feel guilty for all the times I scolded my daughter for the way she was raising her children, and now she's lost her daughter and I can't help feeling awful for the times I scolded her. I blame myself for the pain she is feeling. I would do anything to take her pain away. *I keep saying, "I'm sorry, I'm sorry," but that won't help bring Jessie back or help my daughter's pain. I feel like an additional burden to my daughter, and I can't even say anything to comfort her . . . That's what makes me feel so helpless and useless, and awful.* (Edna)

I pray and pray that God should inflict my son's pain on me so that he might not suffer his child's loss. . . . *I feel like apologizing to my son all the time, as though a part of me knows that it was really my turn to go, but I was selfish and didn't want to go . . . so Josh took my place.* (Dorothy, aged 72 years)

Recovery Process

Some grandparents spoke of their reminiscing and remembering the past and reconciling it with the present as a way of recovering from grief. Others mentioned specific activities which helped them in the recovery process (see italics).

> It is a long road. I had no idea what a long road it was going to be before I was able to forgive myself for living and carrying on when such a young life had been snatched from our midst. For a long time I had a feeling as if something could have been done to prevent his death. Now I don't punish myself anymore by wondering what we could have done to save him. I no longer feel guilty about Randy dying and me, much older, still living. *I write letters to my grandchildren every month, and I write a long one to Randy, my grandson who died, and I look at his pictures. Writing to Randy helps me to feel close to him, and I still tell him to be careful, and to take care of his sisters and his mother.* (Sybil, aged 77 years)

Other grandparents spoke of focusing their thoughts and energies on others and on reorganizing the family interactions and family relations.

> I felt I had been in a cocoon for a while . . . I felt confused and in a daze for a while. Then I realized that it was time to get going. *There were the children to think about, and the other grandchildren whom we had neglected for a while.* We started to get in touch with them and to do the things they enjoyed doing. *It was time to be both parents and grandparents again. Once we thought about it that way, it became easier. We felt we were needed and could be useful.* (Nicholas, aged 57 years)

> The first few months, we felt as if we were each in our own little world, my daughter who lost her girl, and then there's my wife, and the other two grandkids who live in town. We were all very quiet, the grandkids stayed away. Then, a little at a time, my daughter and wife began to talk a bit, and they would stay late at night and talk about our grandchild who died. But I didn't feel much like talking; it was the knowledge that no amount of talking was going to bring him back that kept me very quiet. *For me, I knew I had to get back to work, to become re-engaged in things I'm used to doing, including meetings and office work. The one thing that has changed is that I do now make it a point to spend time with my daughter and son-in-law and her family, and I'm also more concerned with keeping in touch with my sons who live out of town.* I didn't used to contact my son-in-law and sons regularly but our grandchild's death has made me realize that young people who you don't expect will die for a long time, do die. We have to be prepared for the death of young people, too, and we've all got to help each other along, both young and old, parents and grandparents. My son-in-law and I still have little to say to

each other, but I think he knows I'm behind him in his loss. (David, aged 59 years)

Some grandparents spoke of continuing to carry out previously made plans (e.g., travel, work plans), despite the death of the grandchild.

My husband and I had planned to go away . . . you know, we had paid for our trip and so it was close to that time. We didn't know whether to go or not so soon after the child died, but my daughter and I agreed she would be okay, and we should go . . . she said Michael would have wanted us to go. We actually packed with my daughter's help . . . she was wonderfully brave. *We went away on the trip, and although we stayed in touch with my daughter everyday, we felt refreshed. And when we came back we were ready to start all over again with our children and other grandchildren.*

My company had been talking for several months about transferring me to another town, but then this grandson of ours died unexpectedly and I was reluctant to move so soon after his death. My wife, Norah, would not even consider the move, but I didn't want to leave her behind. *So we actually had the movers come and get us moved . . . I am glad we moved. It was a new start for me but it was also very nice that the other grandchildren felt comfortable about visiting us in our new place* . . . it was as if Michael had not been here before, and so it was all right for them to enjoy their stay with us. (Nicholas, aged 57 years)

Changes in Adjusting and Coping Over Time: A Few Commonalities

In the initial stages grandparents struggled considerably with the existential question of whether life was still worthwhile, and whether they would ever overcome the "survivor" guilt that had a grievous impact on their lives. In the earlier in-depth interviews with seventeen grandparents, it was very apparent they blamed themselves considerably for not doing something to save the child, but with the passage of time (i.e., at the time of the 6-month follow-up) grandparents became committed to suppressing their own grief out of their concern to protect their children and surviving grandchildren from further hurt. In the six-month longitudinal follow-up with the grandparents it became increasingly obvious that they felt their first priority was to support their adult children and their families, and to re-engage in family activities that were part of their lives prior to the grandchild's death.

Many times I wondered why I could not have died instead, to save the life of my grandchild and to take away my daughter's pain, *but now I know that it is better if I do not think too much about my own grief, but try to give as much*

> *support as possible to other grieving families, and to my children.* (Sybil, aged 77)

Dorothy, (aged 72), described how she focused on the well-being of other young families in her neighborhood.

> *I slowly became very involved in planning how to help young mothers, and to do things for them and their families that would be helpful and meaningful. I guess that's what sustained me and got me through the times* when I felt so guilty that my young grandchild had been snatched away, and I was still alive but useless to my daughter who lives far away. *I feel that I can get some satisfaction out of being a good grandparent to others' children.* Yes, it is helpful for them, and it helps my daughter, too. I think it is better for her if she doesn't think I am always wanting to be around her, either being too protective of her grief or wanting to talk with her about my grief. I know it is better if I don't think about myself too much or the grandchild, but I still have to know that my daughter is okay.

Other grandparents spoke similarly about effort they had made to focus their thoughts and energies on people and things outside in general to the exclusion of themselves. They spoke of reaching out to others who had lost a child. Two grandmothers whose adult grandchildren committed suicide sought other grieving families to form their own neighborhood reminiscence support group.

At least six grandmothers with whom we had interviews used some form of integrative but public reminiscence with family members and other grieving families in order to reconcile their guilt feelings and regrets, and also to resolve their family's previous conflicts. They also used public reminiscence to achieve a sense of meaning for their own lives by focusing on the special bond they had had with the deceased grandchild. Specifically, the meaning found by these grandmothers in the unique bond with the grandchild was an answer to the question about why the tragic loss occurred. Explanations included references to the endearing qualities of the deceased child, and the potential beneficial effects the death may have had by bringing the family members closer to each other.

Grandmothers, more so than grandfathers, ascribed spiritual significance to the event of the death in a more active way by increasing their own devotion to the family's personal and spiritual growth. Some grandparents described how their spirituality helped to remove the stress they felt in their search for explanations for their grandchild's death.

> *I guess it is because of my faith, I have learned not to ask why this happened to us . . . Over the last six months I don't wonder why the child died. I know there is a reason, and it doesn't matter that I don't know what it is. I accept that, and I accept also that there is a reason I must carry on and be strong for my children's sake.* (Edna)

This spiritual perspective helped Edna in the maintenance of a view that life as a whole was meaningful (i.e., she had to be strong to support her children and surviving grandchildren) even though the traumatic event of the grandchild's death did not hold much meaning.

Another grandmother whose grandchild died around Easter explained how she used religious beliefs to derive a sense of value which she said "sheltered them from the chaos which she initially felt by the tragic event."

> I didn't used to believe in the resurrection before, but it now makes a lot of sense. When the grandchild died, I felt at first it was wicked punishment for the whole family since my grandchild's family were always fighting among themselves. But now I really believe that Trevor's death brought us together to resolve our conflict. He died during holy week. I believe he resurrected our family life. I try to focus on him being with God under a sacred canopy. It helps me to cope with my grief by imagining him resting and relaxing with God. I use this special imagery to deal with his loss.

By comparison, four out of five grandfathers interviewed in the six-month longitudinal follow-up concentrated more on the *functional relevance of tasks* that they felt were helpful to the recovery.

> I have opened a trust account for the education of my two grandchildren. My son has no money to do this, but it is important we rally around the family and make sure the children are well-provided for financially. In any case, there is very little purpose served now in sitting and asking questions about why he died and what we could have done to save him. Over the past six months, I have met with the family financial consultant and I feel much better knowing that the children will be secure financially, and will continue to have all the economic benefits they so truly deserve. My wife and I have lived good lives, but I derive strength from knowing that I am around at this time to help the grandchildren in advice-giving, in assuming responsibility for the major decisions about education and schooling that must be made to secure their future successes. (Nicholas, aged 57)

> It is unrealistic to think that I can shield my son-in-law from the pain of the child's death. For me to attempt to do that will only interfere with the private grief that my son must handle by himself. After a painful four months of wondering what we should do to get over our emotional distress, I decided for myself that it was time to get back to work and get absorbed in it. I feel it has been very healthy for me to do that, and my work has not only increased my social interaction with others, but as a result I feel more able to give emotional support to my son and the family who has lost a child. (David, aged 59)

> I have not always been a very practical man, but after the grandchild died, I realized I had to do a number of quite practical things to help the family

members to pull together. My wife and I decided to assume full responsibility for the care-giving of the other grandchildren, so that my son and daughter-in-law can return to their careers without having to worry about baby-sitting the children. (Philip, aged 72)

One thing I did was to buy us a good computer which has grabbed our attentions and interests. It gives me and my grandchildren and children some activities to do to take our minds off the unhappiness of losing Ronnie. I find the instrumental activities of helping the kids with their homework, teaching them about the computer, and the internet very satisfying. It makes me feel useful to them. I simply cannot get my self to think of the other philosophical questions as to why Ronnie died, who was to blame for it, and what I or anyone else can do about it. I felt over the last six months that it was important that some one take control, and I decided it had to be me. It's the practical things that I have been doing which helped us to recover from our grief. (Ralph, aged 70)

In conclusion, it may be said that with the passage of time, more and more grandparents engaged in interrelated tasks of comprehensibility, manageability, and meaningfulness to cope with their grief. In the recovery process, more women than men experienced a profound deepening of or change in their beliefs about religion and spirituality. More grandmothers, than grandfathers, went through a process of spiritual reappraisal, finally coming to the conclusion that their original beliefs about religion had become stronger and more fully developed as a result of the death of the grandchild.

Grandmothers and grandfathers each struggled individually to make personal choices regarding coping measures they felt were best for them. Grandmothers, more than grandfathers, frequently sought an outlet for emotional expression to deal with their grief, and in the recovery process they offered social support to others to attain emotional healing for themselves. Conversely, grandfathers more frequently than grandmothers, sought an outlet in work activities, and offered practical and instrumental activities to their families, in order to make the grief situation more manageable, controllable, and predictable for themselves. For both sets of grandparents, male and female, the qualitative data showed that there was a noticeable change in beliefs about personal vulnerability. However, this change was experienced by both men and women as wisdom, rather than negativity. In turn all elders acknowledged that this wisdom guided them in new ways of relating to their family members.

DISCUSSION

The present investigation was an initial attempt to identify major themes underlying the grief and bereavement of grandparents as related to the deceased grandchild and other members of the family. The factor analyses results provided documented data about the major factors, including specific items describing long-term grief reactions of grandparents.

Some of the important themes which emerged concerning the grandparents' grief and related concerns have clear implications for health providers and bereavement counselors. Principal among these are the strong sense of "survivor guilt." This finding, replicated also in the qualitative data collected for the study, corroborates the observations of previous researchers and writers [e.g., 24-26] who have commented on the extreme anguish that older adults feel about the grave untimeliness of the death of a young child.

Another significant factor which emerged in the factor analyses results and was clearly reflected also in the qualitative analyses was the grandparents' immediate sense of helplessness and pain arising from their desire to shield their adult child against the pain and hurt of losing a child. Regardless of how well the grandparent knew the deceased grandchild, it is obvious that the grandparent was willing to put aside his or her own pain to alleviate the pain of the adult child with whom there was the continuity of a strong biosocial life. This finding supports the observations of Moss, Lesher, and Moss [17] who note that the image of a deceased child is tied up in the historical self of the parent. Grandparents may feel doubly bereaved; not only do they feel grief because they have been bereft of their grandchild, but they also have to contend with the grief they feel because of their inability to shield their adult children from the pain and loss of their child. In the present study, the inability to help or be useful to the family members in the hour of grief often increased the feelings of hopelessness and helplessness that many grandparents experienced. As confirmed several times, especially in the qualitative data, the sense of "survivor guilt" may be aggravated by the sense of uselessness that grandparents feel toward their adult child in helping with the grief. Both in the qualitative and quantitative analyses, it is implicit that whenever a family member dies, it is frequently the grandparents who feel an urgent need to realign their relationships and patterns of interaction with members of the family. We can only speculate about what the grandparents feel about their responsibility as grandparents. However, there is sufficient data in the present study to suggest that especially during a difficult time of death and family bereavement, grandparents continue with greater perseverance in their role as "family watchdogs" [27]. The findings of the present study suggest that when a grandchild dies, the grandparents are subsumed by their responsibility as a parent to the adult child. If there is a chance to fulfill this responsibility, it would appear that their next concern seems to be with caring for and nurturing their living grandchildren and realigning relationships with other family members. Thus, one predominant message that emerges from the data is that the dissynchrony expressed by parents who have lost a child [see 28-30] is mirrored and often amplified by grandparents who, at the end of their lives, are struggling with the untimeliness of the death of the grandchild, both for themselves and their adult child.

The results raise some important questions concerning the parameters of grief and the dynamics of their interactions with all members of the grieving family. The study provides excellent data for generating hypotheses for future research. Some generalizations with respect to the "survivor guilt" and the continuing need that grandparents have to give their children's grief first priority are very valid, but may nevertheless be warranted only in a limited way, primarily due to the limitations in our sampling procedures. The sample was one of convenience—not a random one. Most of the participants were volunteers who had lost a grandchild, and 72 percent of the participants were females. At the time of recruitment of participants, the ages of the deceased grandchildren had not been precisely determined by the researcher. The details of this information became available over the course of several months following the recruitment of participants. Neither was specific information available as to how long ago the death of the grandchild had occurred. Some of this information about the ages of the deceased grandchildren, their gender, and year of death was subsequently gleaned through later telephone queries and at the time of the in-depth interviews with some of the grandparents. Hence, several other statistical comparisons pertaining to the recovery process were not planned in the research design. The qualitative data reported in the study, however, were obtained from interviewing only those grandparents whose grandchild had died recently (i.e., 6 months or less prior to the time of the study). A six-month longitudinal follow-up was conducted with respect to tracing the recovery process for twelve grandmothers and five grandfathers. As the results of Study 2 revealed, the qualitative data were most useful in elucidating the precise coping strategies and ego-defenses that elderly grandparents used to surmount the intense reactions of grief following the loss of a grandchild.

Despite some of the obvious limitations of the research arising from using a convenience sample, the present study has a number of unique features which may be used, with advantage, in future research. Predominant among these, is that it is one of the few studies that documents empirical data and draws attention to normative dimensions of the grief reactions as derived from a systematic factor analysis procedure. Another unique feature of the present investigation is the attempt to combine a quantitative and qualitative approach to data collection. There are a number of ways in which qualitative and quantitative data can be linked [31, 32], but the current investigation of grandparents' grief reactions relied mostly on the method of triangulation [33]. This essentially involved considering statistical data alongside quotes from individual subjects that were selected to illustrate the main themes suggested by the statistical data.

An important advantage of our qualitative data, although drawn from a limited group of seventeen participants, is that the qualitative data helped us to further clarify our understanding of the quantitative data and the extrapolations from statistical data. A third unique feature of the study is that our qualitative approach to understanding the heterogeneity of participants' responses also included a *six-month follow-up component* which helped us to be more sensitive to the conditions and variables that contribute to the *recovery process* in late life bereavement.

Although decisions about methodology in research on bereavement and grief ought to be considered in relation to the questions being asked by researchers, our recommendation is that the ideal investigatory approach would be one in which the quantitative and qualitative methods are best used together, since each can serve to be a confirmatory analysis of the other. The success of the factor analytic procedures in identifying a number of interpretable factors in the grief reactions of elderly grandparents over the loss of a grandchild supports Wade's [34] recommendation that combinations of questionnaires and structured interviews may be more promising instruments for future research with elderly persons than questionnaires alone. The use of in-depth interviews with individuals, allowing them sufficient flexibility to reminisce and provide a personal narrative of dominant thoughts, feelings and behaviors in which they engaged immediately after the loss, and in the course of several months following the loss, makes this study different from other clinical studies by professionals who may interject their own biased interpretations. Certainly, future research is needed in a general population of parents who have suffered the loss of a child, and subsequently, to compare parents' grief reactions with those of grandparents. Such research is particularly warranted with respect to factors of "Survivor Guilt," "Need to Restructure Relationship With Family Members," and "Recovery Process" which emerged quite clearly in the present investigation of grandparents' grief reactions.

ACKNOWLEDGMENTS

Grateful thanks are extended to the Kerby Centre in Calgary for assistance in connecting with various seniors' agencies and seniors' day-care centres for recruitment of subjects in Calgary and the outlying districts of Airdrie, Cochrane, Crossfield, High River, Lethbridge and Red Deer, Alberta. The help of research assistant, Evelyn Doyle, in recruitment of subjects and data collection is especially appreciated. Charlene Batlowski assisted in tabulation and organization of data files, and Dr. Mark Koledziej helped with preliminary statistical procedures used in the quantitative data analysis. Special thanks are extended to the volunteer subjects who responded to the questionnaire and others who agreed to be interviewed and shared with us their stressful experiences.

REFERENCES

1. T. Hartshorne and G. Manaster, The Relationship with Grandparents: Contact, Importance, Role Conception, *International Journal of Aging and Human Development, 15*, pp. 233-245, 1982.

2. E. Timberlake, The Value of Grandchildren to Grandmothers, *Journal of Gerontological Social Work, 3*, pp. 63-76, 1980.
3. C. Barranti, The Grandparent/Grandchild Relationship: Family Resources in an Era of Voluntary Bonds, *Family Relations, 34*, pp. 343-352, 1985.
4. J. Ponzetti, Bereaved Families: A Comparison of Parents' and Grandparents' Reactions to the Death of a Child, *Omega: Journal of Death and Dying, 25*, pp. 63-71, 1992.
5. J. Ponzetti and M. Johnson, The Forgotten Grievers: Grandparents' Reactions to the Death of Grandchildren, *Death Studies, 15*, pp. 157-167, 1991.
6. N. Wedemeyer, Transformation of Family Images Related to Death, *Journal of Family Issues, 7*, pp. 337-351, 1986.
7. M. S. Link, The Grandparenting Role, *Lifestyles: A Journal of Changing Patterns, 8*, pp. 27-34, 1987.
8. B. L. Neugarten and K. K. Weinstein, The Changing American Grandparent, *Journal of Marriage and the Family, 26*, pp. 199-204, 1964.
9. J. L. Thomas, The Development of Grandparents' Relationships with Their Grandchildren: A Qualitative Study, Doctoral Dissertation, West Virginia University, *Dissertation Abstracts International, 43*, pp. 4211-4205B, 1982.
10. J. L. Thomas, Age and Sex Differences in Perceptions of Grandparenting, *Journal of Gerontology, 41*, pp. 417-423, 1986.
11. J. L. Thomas, Gender and Perceptions of Grandparenthood, *International Journal of Aging and Human Development, 29*:4, pp. 269-282, 1989.
12. D. L. Gutmann, Parenthood: Key to Comparative Study of the Life Cycle, in *Life-Span Developmental Psychology: Normative Life Crises*, N. Datan and L. Ginsberg (eds.), Academic Press, New York, 1975.
13. J. Gyulay, The Forgotten Grievers, *American Journal of Nursing, 75*, pp. 1476-1479, 1978.
14. R. Kalish, Older People and Grief, *Generations, 11*, pp. 33-38, 1987.
15. J. L. Thomas, Grandparenthood and Mental Health: Implications for the Practitioner, *Journal of Applied Gerontology, 9*:4, pp. 464-479, 1990.
16. H. Q. Kivnick, Grandparenthood: An Overview of Meaning and Mental Health, *The Gerontologist, 22*, pp. 59-66, 1982.
17. M. Moss, E. Lesher, and S. Moss, Impact of the Death of an Adult Child on Elderly Parents: Some Observations, *Omega: Journal of Death and Dying, 17*, pp. 209-218, 1986-87.
18. I. Levav, Mortality and Psychopathology following the Death of an Adult Child: An Epidemiological Review, *Israel Journal of Psychiatry and Related Sciences, 19*, pp. 23-38.
19. B. L. Neugarten, Adaptation and the Life Cycle, *Journal of Geriatric Psychiatry, 4*, pp. 71-87, 1970.
20. S. Folkman, R. S. Lazarus, S. Pimley, and J. Novacek, Age Differences in Stress and Coping Processes, *Psychology and Aging, 2*, pp. 171-184, 1987.
21. H. F. Kaiser, An Index of Factorial Simplicity, *Psychometrika, 39*, pp. 31-36, 1974.
22. J. O. Kim and C. W. Mueller, *Factor Analysis: Statistical Methods and Practical Issues*, Sage, Beverly Hills, 1978.
23. R. B. Cattell, Factor Analysis: An Introduction to Essentials, *Biometrics, 21*, pp. 190-215; 405-435, 1965.

24. T. Rando, *Grieving: How to go on Living When Someone You Love Dies*, Lexington Books, Lexington, Massachusetts, 1988.
25. I. Videka-Sherman, Coping with the Death of a Child: A Study Overtime, *American Journal of Orthopsychiatry, 52*, pp. 688-698, 1982.
26. J. Hamilton, Grandparents as Grievers, in *The Child and Death*, O. J. Sahler (ed.), Mosby, St. Louis, pp. 219-225, 1978.
27. L. Troll, Grandparenting, in *Aging in the 1980s: Psychological Issues*, L. Poon (ed.), American Psychological Association, Washington, D.C., 1980.
28. R. Knapp, *Beyond Endurance: When a Child Dies*, Schocken Books, New York, 1986.
29. M. Miles and E. Crandal, The Search for Meaning and its Potential for Affecting Growth in Bereaved Parents, in *Coping with Life Crisis: An Integrated Approach*, R. H. Moos (ed.), Plenum, New York, pp. 235-243, 1986.
30. T. Rando, Bereaved Parents: Particular Difficulties, Unique Factors, and Treatment Issues, *Social Work, 30*, pp. 19-23, 1985.
31. M. B. Miles and A. M. Huberman, *Qualitative Data Analysis: A Sourcebook of New Methods*, Sage, California, 1984.
32. M. Q. Patton, *Creative Evaluation*, Sage, California, 1981.
33. J. McCartney, Addictive Behaviors: Relationship Factors and Their Perceived Influence on Change, *Genetic, Social and General Psychology Monographs, 121*:1, pp. 39-64, 1995.
34. P. Wade, Factor Analytic Approaches to the Investigation of Common Fears: A Critical Appraisal and Reanalysis, *Behavior Therapy, 9*, pp. 923-935, 1978.

KINSHIP BEREAVEMENT IN LATER LIFE: UNDERSTANDING VARIATIONS IN CAUSE, COURSE, AND CONSEQUENCE

BRIAN DE VRIES
University of British Columbia and
San Francisco State University, California

ABSTRACT

This discussion directs itself to a review and synthesis of the chronicles of later life kinship loss as presented in this volume. Several efforts are aimed in this direction. First, four broad generalizations about bereavement are offered: 1) Bereavement is a complex experience, 2) influenced by the context within which the loss takes place as well as 3) the nature of the lost relationship and the role the deceased played, 4) with an endpoint that is variable and unclear. The particular influences of specific losses are also addressed. Second, the empirical issues corresponding to these generalizations are discussed as are the more substantive issues of the appraisal of the loss, the role(s) of gender, and the influence of spirituality. Finally, the application of these works are identified and framed in the context of later life bereavement.

The six articles in this volume sample the varied and vast domain of bereavement with results attesting to the many and significant effects of loss. New insights have been afforded by these investigations and previous results have been replicated. The aim of this concluding article is to review some of these results through highlighting what may be said about bereavement in general, specific types of loss in particular, and the approaches researchers take to these issues. Some concluding thoughts touch on the applications of these findings for those whose empirical and/or personal agendas include understanding the process of bereavement.

© 1997, Baywood Publishing Co., Inc.

GENERALIZATIONS ABOUT BEREAVEMENT

At least four broad generalizations about bereavement may be offered drawing from the foregoing accounts: 1) Bereavement is a complex experience, 2) influenced by the context within which the loss takes place as well as 3) the nature of the lost relationship and the role the deceased played, 4) with an endpoint that is variable and unclear. An explication of these generalization follows.

1. Bereavement is a Complex Experience

Statements characterizing bereavement as a complex phenomenon are neither new [e.g., 1-3] nor particularly surprising given the enormous and far-reaching impact personal relationships have on our daily lives. The scope of this multiplicity, however, continues to unfold [4-6] as it has in the accounts represented in this volume which attest to the multidimensionality and multidirectionality of bereavement and the multiple levels on which adaptation takes place.

The *multidimensionality* of bereavement and bereavement reactions is demonstrated here both in the accounts of the diversity of losses suffered and by the range of domains affected by such deaths. A growing body of research supports the conclusion that bereavement exacts a toll on psychological and physical health across loss types. Depression and other expressions of sadness are common; so too are decrements in abilities to perform activities of daily living and perceived health and even elevated rates of mortality. A host of secondary and concomitant stressors and anxieties are also frequently identified as a result of the loss including changes in one's social, financial, and physical environment. Guilt frequently accompanies loss and may derive from simply being a survivor (e.g., when a younger life has *prematurely* ended) or from not providing the care and/or attention that one could or *should* have provided. Changes in levels of satisfaction with and concerns about current and ongoing relationships are also noted. Thoughts of the deceased may intrude on daily functioning or may serve to keep memories of a loved one active and present. Changes in one's assumptions of life and fundamental beliefs (including religion) may arise as individuals attempt to impose order on what might otherwise appear as aleatoric. Less frequently targeted, but nonetheless noteworthy, domains influenced by bereavement include issues of self-image and identity and a related sense of personal finitude and connectedness to others.

Implicit in many of these latter dimensions of bereavement is evidence of the *multidirectional* nature of their influence (e.g., increases in relationship satisfaction in the face of personal sadness; both intrusive and comforting thoughts of the deceased). Bereavement research in general, and the study of spousal loss in particular, has largely centered its efforts on the assessment of depression [e.g., 7], excluding analyses of other outcomes, both positive and negative [8, 9] or even a type of emotional neutrality. As Arbuckle and de Vries [10] suggest, however, the experience and knowledge of surviving one of life's most traumatic events, of having endured such pain, may serve to enhance a sense of self-confidence and self-efficacy, a sort of "crisis competence" [11]. The comparable forms of enhancement or efficacy reported herein included the *greater* marital satisfaction of bereaved parents (perhaps a growing together in grief), the relatively *positive* appraisal of the loss of a sibling (perhaps framed in terms of altruism or social comparison, i.e., relief concerning the end of another's suffering or an appreciation of one's own fate given the fate of others) and the sources of *wisdom* described by bereaved grandparents guiding them in new ways of relating to family members.

Yet another aspect of this complexity, revealed in the foregoing studies, concerns the *multiple levels* on which adaptation to bereavement takes place. This is most clearly documented in Bower's analysis of the language of acceptance of the death of an elderly parent. The words with which we recount our experiences (or the words we omit in initial reports, as was the case in at least one of Prigerson et al.'s respondents) not only represent themes of understanding, they also suggest a certain structure of thinking. The perceived and compelling need to explain at some length reactions to and beliefs about the death represents yet another level of analysis, perhaps addressing social values or norms. As a further complicating factor, behavior (including body posture and movements, for example) may belie the words and sentiment being expressed. In similarly subtle terms, bereaved and nonbereaved parents identify comparable numbers of sources of life satisfaction and worry, yet weight and order these sources differently. Both researchers and clinicians might best serve their populations by attending to and addressing the multiple dimensions, directions and levels by which bereavement in general may be characterized.

In addition to this overall complexity common to many of the losses described above, several unique challenges have been discussed in conjunction with particular losses and deserve attention here as a point of contrast. As intimated in the accounts presented by Prigerson et al., and echoed in the spousal bereavement literature [see 2, 10, 12, 13], widowed persons undergo emotional and cognitive *reformations to the new role of a single person*, accompanied by necessarily altered routines and rhythms of daily living with frequent reductions in financial and social resources. Brothers and sisters see in the death of their sibling the *manifestation of their own genetic legacy* as Hays et al. report; the family role and personal future of the self is made salient in the death of a sibling. Adult (and mostly middle-aged) children similarly experience a change in their personal meaning of time and death following the death of their parent [e.g., 14], and may engage in a crude form of calculus seeing in the death intimations of their own mortality [15]. They also report an awareness of their *"omega generation" group membership* [16] and "middle-aged orphan[hood]" [17], although they struggle to maintain a tie with the deceased as Moss et al. and Bower discuss. Parents speak of an acute sense of lost order as young lives end before their "rightful time." Parents particularly report a sense of violation and increased feelings of uselessness and an *existential loss of meaning and purpose* in life with enduring effects on personal functioning. In our discussion with bereft parents [e.g., 18], a sort of untethered existence was described as the grounding link between the past and the future was severed. The grandparents in Fry's study articulate the *generative and multiple sources of their grief* [see also 19, 20] in their deep sorrow for the lost future of their deceased grandchild, their empathy for their adult children and their own efforts to suppress their grief so as not to further burden others.

These unique challenges offer interesting and telling insights into the experiences of particular groups of bereft adults identifying the trajectories and substance of grief as well as the core issues and understanding of relationships. The extent to which these challenges are specific to loss types remains an empirical question worthy of pursuit.

2. Bereavement Occurs in a Context

That bereavement takes place in a personal and socio-historical context [see 21-23] is a point infrequently articulated in perspectives on loss. Averill and Nunley have pointed out, for example, that emotional reactions to bereavement cannot be isolated from other social and personal reactions and the course of time during which such responses unfold [21]. de Vries et al. make this point directly [see also 10]. The death of an adult child is a loss disproportionately manifested in the lives of those whose resources may already be compromised—that is, more women than men, more older than younger parents, more widowed than married individuals, more African Americans than other racial groups, and more lower than higher SES individuals. As Lopata has suggested, this social and demographic profile may undermine an individual's ability and opportunity to clarify problems, identify available resources and take action in the service of possible solutions [12]. These "covariates" merit more "main effect" attention.

The context of bereavement is also alluded to by the other articles in diverse ways. Prigerson et al., for example, provocatively discuss some of the personality and other factors that may predispose individuals to more traumatic grief, including an unstable self-image, unstable affect, and separation-induced anxiety. The links between anticipatory grief and subsequent traumatic grief make these predisposing factors even more salient. The cause of the death has been identified in at least a couple of analyses as a relevant factor, although the role of cause of death in bereavement reactions has frequently yielded equivocal results, particularly in the literature on spousal bereavement [e.g., 2]. The death, however, may well have occurred in the context of other illnesses, accidents, or incidents which may influence responses, as Bower suggests. Moss et al. also point out that the death of the second parent (in comparison with the death of the first parent) exerts an influence on the adult child's reactions, particularly a sense of "orphanhood."

This latter point raises the more general issues of previous losses and bereavement experiences, something to which researchers rarely attend. de Vries et al. and Hays et al. both compare their bereaved samples to random samples of relevantly-constituted non-bereaved. Perhaps this is an issue of semantics only, but the non-bereaved nature of these controls is quite narrowly defined (i.e., either by a *specific* loss or a relatively brief and *particular period of* time). In fact, the bereaved nature of the target groups in all of these (and most other) studies may be said to be similarly narrowly defined. That is, few individuals reach their later years without enduring the death of several, if not many or even all [e.g., 24], significant persons. Along such lines, Kastenbaum has described a "bereavement overload" arising from a succession of losses over time resulting in a cumulative effect with particular vulnerabilities [25]. Moss and Moss have suggested that the experience of family deaths over a lifetime create a persistent "personal pool of grief" that intensifies with each additional loss [14]. These previous encounters with death provide a framework for the current bereavement experience of individuals and, in conjunction with characteristics of the death and the characteristics of the individuals who grieve, represent a salient and neglected aspect of reactions to loss.

3. Bereavement is Influenced by the Nature of the Lost Relationship and the Role the Deceased Played

Implicit in a contextual accounting of bereavement is knowledge of the nature of the lost relationship and the role the deceased played in the lives of those now left to grieve. This salience of this dimension, however, is reflected in a variety of ways in all of the articles in this volume and merits special attention [see also 26].

In the qualitative accounts, the bereft themselves repeatedly and poignantly alluded to the nature of the relationship lost through death and the role the deceased played. Recall, for example, Mr. Rs traumatic grief following the death of his "bashert" through whom he maintained and enhanced his identity (Prigerson et al.). Recall, also, the grandmother (Wilma) in Fry's study who described her deceased grandson and her devastated dreams of and for him as follows: "His parents and we had so many hopes for him, we even joked with him about how he could look after us . . . and now he's gone." And, finally, remember Bower's forty-six-year-old caregiving daughter bereft of her father who voiced her lonely emptiness at not being needed in the following: "Like, I'm still thinking: Oh, well. I have to go fix Daddy's pills. I got to make dinner for Daddy . . . And I look, and the house is so dark and lonely. And I think: What am I doing?"

These quotes reveal part of what the grievers perceive to have lost and hint at the nature of their lost relationships.

The above-noted authors explicitly address this link between these affective and functional aspects of the lost relationship and the reactions to the death. Prigerson et al. conclude that attachment concepts (i.e., knowledge of the working models of the affectional relationship) are useful in understanding the genesis of traumatic grief, particularly as it applies to the spouses in their article; the association between anticipatory and traumatic grief further attests to the importance of knowledge of the prior relationship. In a similar way, Fry calls upon the literature on diversity in grandparenthood roles [e.g., 27] to draw attention to the varying ties between grandparents and their grandchildren as well as the embeddedness of grandparents in family relationships and the potential implication of such variance for the grief and bereavement of grandparents. Bower reports that some adult children come to an acceptance of death when it is warranted by an understood and sometimes welcome end to a lengthy illness, a lengthy relationship or even a lengthy life, all of which also implicate relationship function and quality.

The strength of the measures of continuing tie with the deceased parent (in Moss et al.'s study) further testifies to the importance of knowledge regarding the previous and ongoing relationship between parent and child. Also noteworthy in this context is the magnitude and consistency of relationship quality measures as well as measures addressing the amount and type of care that the parent received prior to her or his death in the prediction of bereavement outcomes. These measures reflect the roles that have been played and the nature of the relationship bond. de Vries et al. draw a similar conclusion in discussing the modestly stronger bereavement effect associated with the death of a daughter. Largely, however, they lament the absence of information on the nature and function of the lost relationship, as do Hays et al. In fact, Hays et al. make this point most strongly reminding readers of the variability in sibling relationships [e.g., over the life course, by gender, by personality and/or attachment style; see 28-30] and the utility of such information in bereavement theory development and hypothesis-testing. The comments above reveal some of the benefits of access to such information and stand as further support for calls for attention to this level of important detail.

4. The Endpoint of Bereavement is Both Variable and Unclear

Perhaps the grounds of greatest discrepancy in the articles of this volume entail discussions of the definition and timing of the endpoint of bereavement. This is a discrepancy that can be found in almost any compilation of articles in the bereavement literature. The predominant view in the literature is echoed in the words of Stroebe and Stroebe [31, p. 121] who write that "after twelve to eighteen months most bereaved begin to recover and ultimately show little sign of psychological damage." In contrast, Wortman and Silver have commented on the extent of variations in reactions to the loss of a loved one and have questioned "normal" reactions to bereavement in any specified time frame and "recovery" from the same [8, 9]. For example, Lehman, Wortman, and Williams [32] report bereavement effects of up to four years in duration, extended to up to fifteen years in Arbuckle and de Vries [10] and even then, may be only partial or incomplete [33]. Inquiries into the identification and presence of the endpoint of bereavement remain open and unanswered.

Bower confronted this issue most directly questioning both the meaning and measurement of acceptance as the end of grief's course, including its conceptual overlap with terms such as recognition, resignation, and resolution. In the voices of the bereft adult children of Bower's sample, 90 percent reported having accepted the death of their last surviving parent within a period of six- to eight-month period of time. The heavily explained nature of this acceptance, however, may pose some challenges to this acceptance and merits further attention. The larger sample of adult children in Moss et al.'s study also scored high on level of acceptance (on a scale constructed by the authors), although this was more true for men than it was for women. These same adult children, however, also reported moderately high levels of grief and *ongoing* tie with the deceased; what does this indicate about "recovery?"

The siblings in Hays et al.'s report were bereft for a period of time up to and including one year, although time since the death did not figure prominently into any analyses. Within this window of time, bereavement effects were noted particularly in the domains of physical health and cognition, although the effects were fewer and somewhat less dramatic than were predicted. Furthermore, in the absence of longitudinal data, inferences cannot be drawn about the evolution of this bereavement and hence its trajectory or route to recovery. Within the three years of time since the death, and over the six months of the study, the bereaved grandparents in Fry's study commented on their recovery process, including their gradual reintegration into social networks and social activities. Of particular importance to these grandparents was the suppressing of their own grief over time to allow them the strength and opportunity to protect their children and surviving grandchildren. Fry refers to these tasks as ones of comprehensibility, manageability, and meaningfulness as ways in which these grandparents *continue* to cope with their grief.

de Vries et al. found evidence of both differences and consistency in their comparisons of bereaved parents up to ten years following the death of their adult child with non-bereaved controls; many of these effects remained over the two waves of study, while others increased in magnitude. Although modest in both size and number, these effects nonetheless underscore the depth of the impact of the loss and the ongoing struggle depicted by these parents. Such a struggle was perhaps most clearly represented in the shorter-term traumatic bereavement reactions presented by Prigerson et al. where symptoms evidenced in response to loss meet the stipulation for *chronic* Post-Traumatic Stress Disorder.

Indeed, the course of bereavement is variable and leads to an ambiguous endpoint. It has been suggested elsewhere that there may be losses from which individuals do not recover (e.g., the death of an adult child, see [34]) or, alternatively, losses which generate little grief (e.g., the death of a friend or other "community" member, see [33]). Other accounts have been presented here suggesting more individual difference levels of analysis (e.g., traumatic grief). Perhaps the safe summary is to suggest that recovery (or adaptation or accommodations, e.g., [10]) is not a single indicator [see 33] and end this discussion where it began with reference to the complex and multidimensional nature of bereavement.

EMPIRICAL ISSUES IN BEREAVEMENT

A survey of the approaches taken, and results presented, in the articles of this volume offer an opportunity to address a variety of issues of importance to the *study* of bereavement. Several of these are issues of measurement, previously introduced in the discussions surrounding the generalizations and augmented below in an order corresponding to their initial presentation. The substantive issues of gender, appraisal, and spirituality form the second detail of the following section.

Measurement Issues

The complex nature of bereavement has natural implications for its study including the use of multiple indicators of adaptation [33, 35], some of which address the potential for positive affect and growth in the face of trauma [e.g., 10, 36], and the subtle yet profound levels on which change may occur. Thematic and structural analyses of the language used by the bereft themselves have been offered as approaches in this latter regard (i.e., Bower's article). An issue superordinate to these, however, called for in almost every article of this collection and articulated most clearly in the work of Fry, is the combination of both quantitative and qualitative data. The conjoint consideration of statistical information (based on reliable and well-validated measures enabling comparisons across studies) along side illuminating text both illustrates and reinforces primary themes in responses.

The context within which the loss takes place was described above with measurement suggestions including the assessment of personality characteristics and previous bereavement experiences, perhaps part of the personal-historical context of the individual griever, in addition to her or his social and demographic profile. Lund and others have written that such socio-economic indicators appears to have minimal effects on spousal bereavement adjustment measures; with different forms of loss, however, the role of these data has yet to be fully tested [2]. The results of the studies reported here offer promise in this effort as seen in the variables of education, income (partially reviewed above) and gender (addressed below). Life course variations in bereavement are currently being discussed [4, 5] with suggestions that older survivors may experience greater distress as they also cope with age-related personal, health, and social losses [37] in addition to the loss of a relationship of probably longer duration with a greater interdependent [6] and affectively-richer base [38]. The role of ethnicity and/or race in bereavement reactions is a relatively open question also offering the promise of fine and important distinctions [e.g., 39].

An important aspect of the context of bereavement is the nature of the lost relationship and the role the deceased played in the life of the griever. All losses are not the same and, in accordance with Lieberman [6], there is a need to understand both the common and specific challenges faced by the survivors of different family losses. In this regard, cases have already been made for the inclusion of information on relationship style and attachment status (e.g., between spouses as in Prigerson et al.'s article) and solidarity or intimacy measures (e.g., between grandparent and grandchild as in Fry's article and between siblings as discussed by Hays et al.) describing the relationship between the bereft and the deceased prior to death. These examples, however, issue a broader and secondary message in that they are framed in the theory-driven terms of the relationship (and loss) under investigation, a framing that is all too uncommon in bereavement research. That is, if grief and bereavement represent "the study of individuals and their most intimate relationships" [40, p. 80], then it follows that researchers would explore and draw from the burgeoning literatures on particular relationships (such as spousal, grandparent-grandchild, and sibling relationships), in addition to the bereavement literature, to inform their studies on particular relationship losses. This effectively introduces literature-defining relational measures to analysis of bereavement and explorations of grief and bereavement to the study of relationships informing both the meaning and experience of relationships and the meaning of their loss [41].

Assuming a variable course and consequence of bereavement has several implications for analysis. For example, adoption of such a perspective should shed implicit limits on the range of empirical investigations; that is, few studies explore bereavement reactions beyond one year following the loss [see 32; and de Vries et al., this issue, for reviews]. Even fewer examine (or have access to) prospective data which might anchor pre-death trajectories of grief and bereavement; longitudinal investigations of caregivers provide the forum and opportunity for such analyses. Correspondingly, one need not assume a linear process or a lack of variation within and between the multiple dimensions. Instead, as Arbuckle and de Vries [10] and others have claimed, bereavement may be characterized as periods of overlapping and alternating intervals of searching, anger, guilt, anxiety, sadness, and depression [21, 35] as well as feelings of relief and pride associated with coping and moments of happiness [36, 42]. Perhaps the more manageable goal in bereavement research might be to better understand and characterize the sources of the variation inherent in the process and the players.

Substantive Issues

Appraisals of Loss (and Recovery)

The stress and coping framework [43] has been a fairly popular heuristic for studies on bereavement, with the death interpreted as the stressful event and reactions to the death as exemplars of ways of coping. The centerpiece of this framework is the individual's appraisal of what is at stake in the event, helping to define the parameters of the stressor and the coping responses. This important subjective and evaluative information about what has been lost, *i.e., the meaning of the death (and the self-assessed course and nature of recovery)*, has been noticeably absent from much of the bereavement research, perhaps attributable to the loose application of this framework to the study of loss. It is surprising how rarely the voices of the bereft are heard as reporters of their own experience.

Several articles in this volume have attempted to redress this imbalance through giving voice to the bereft in a variety of ways. Bower's article does so most pointedly in her efforts to explore what the bereaved mean by acceptance of the death, finding that acceptance is more than the return of ordinary levels of functioning or the absence of depressive symptomatology (i.e., those indicators most frequently identified by researchers). Prigerson et al. provide illustrative accounts of what the relationships meant to those whose grief has taken a complicated course. Fry, too, presents examples of relationship meaning and the spontaneous reference to process of adaptation and reasons for recovery.

The studies of a more quantitative nature have also attempted to include some evaluative measure (e.g., the question in Hays et al.'s study on the "effect of the death" on respondents and the self-rated recovery index in de Vries et al.), with modest success. The few relationships between the self-rated recovery responses and other bereavement measures, as well as the intriguing but inconclusive nature of one death having a more positive effect than another, leave open the door for multiple interpretations—interpretations best made by those whose lives have been altered by the loss. The previous calls for combinations of quantitative and qualitative data are echoed in these remarks as researchers are encouraged to uncover what individuals report as the substance of their grief, how this varies over time and when (and if) they draw some line signaling its conclusion.

Gender

The role of gender, as played out in the literature on personal and social relationships, has been surprisingly complex and the subject of substantial debate [e.g., 44-46]; its role may be comparably described in explorations of bereavement, particularly as revealed here. Lund has reviewed the literature on spousal bereavement in later life and has reported that although men and women experience some aspects of grief differently, they are more similar than dissimilar on the global indicators of loss-related emotions and behaviors [2]. An analogous summary may be made of the studies in this volume in that, when explored in this "main effect" manner, gender differences on the global and central indicators were mostly statistically weak. However, the studies reported herein offer the opportunity to explore iterations of gender pairings unavailable in studies of spousal loss. That is, in the spousal bereavement literature, wives have lost husbands and husbands have lost wives. In other accounts of loss as presented above, grandfathers and grandmothers have lost granddaughters and grandsons, mothers and fathers have lost sons and daughters, daughters and sons have lost fathers and mothers, brothers and sisters have lost sisters and brothers.

These iterations have manifested themselves in several provocative examples of bereavement reactions. Most pronounced in this respect are the result presented by Moss et al. revealing patterns of results differing for the children of mothers in contrast to fathers on some measures, for sons in contrast to daughters on others, and for combinations of these two (e.g., contrasts between sons of deceased mothers and daughters of deceased fathers or daughters of deceased mothers *and* fathers in contrast to sons of deceased mothers) on still other measures. Although less pronounced, Hays et al. also report interesting differences distinguishing bereaved sisters from brothers: the loss of a brother was related to increased depressive symptomatology for sisters more so than the loss of a sister; the loss of a brother had greater financial repercussions for brothers than for surviving sisters. On a more suggestive level, de Vries et al. report that the death of a daughter, as opposed to a son, was weakly associated with a self-perceived failure to recover; this result falls generally into the realm of previous research which has reported higher levels of distress with the death of a child of the same sex as the grieving parent [e.g., 47, 48]. Together, these results suggest exciting directions for future research and call for increased attention to the potential effects of gender particularly as it varies in the dyad of the deceased and the bereft.

Spirituality and Religious Beliefs

Lund, and others, has commented on the weak relationship between religion and most major indicators of bereavement outcomes as revealed in a number of studies of later life spousal loss, and at least one of the studies reported herein (i.e., Moss et al.) [2]. The puzzling nature of this pattern of findings remains open for discussion, but may result at least in part from issues of measurement. That is, religion and the beliefs comprised therein, are more than number of times one attends church, engages in some religious activity or even prays. The more implicit and subtle nature of religion and spirituality are suggested by several of the analyses reported in this volume.

For example, Bower reports that parental death was regarded as God's will for several adult children. The effects of advanced age, terminal illness and even death itself was seen as having developed according to God's plan. The role of God's will and issues of spirituality, however, were also evident in the theme of "Death as Endpoint," where the death was accepted as a divine and moral transaction or God's reclamation. This reclamation was seen as particularly cruel by Prigerson et al.'s Mr. R who exhibited conflicted feelings of rage and guilt at God for taking back the gift of his wife.

Several of the grandparents in Fry's study, and grandmothers in particular, ascribed spiritual significance to the death of their grandchild from which they derived comfort and value. These individuals claimed assistance in coping by "imagining [the grandchild] resting and relaxing with God" (as reported by one grandmother) as well as reductions in the overall stress associated with the loss. Similarly, de Vries et al. found that bereaved mothers were more likely to mention religion as a source of satisfaction or pleasure in their lives. These results are suggestive of the background and perhaps framing role played by religion, spirituality and/or other belief systems and its even more complex role as mediated by gender and perhaps other factors as well.

IMPLICATIONS AND APPLICATIONS

Embedded in the generalizations about bereavement and the empirical issues described above are several implications for those whose personal and/or professional lives bring them into contact with the elderly bereft. Perhaps the superordinate statement to be made in this respect is that notwithstanding the commonalities that may appear in responses to loss, all bereavement is not alike just as all grievers are not alike. The universal course of bereavement has yet to be determined.

Some of the unique challenges confronted by those who have lost a spouse, a sibling, a parent, a child, or a grandchild have been previously reviewed and implicate areas of particular sensitivity for supporters of the bereft. These include: identity and attachment issues for bereaved spouses; an increased risk of morbidity and poorer perceived health for siblings; a sense of personal finitude and temporal reorientation for adult children; an existential loss of meaning and purpose in life for older parents; and the survival guilt and generative suppression of grief characteristic of grandparents. As suggested above, these challenges may be exacerbated or modified in other ways by the quality and nature of the lost relationship. Prigerson et al., for example, found that unusually good marriages were more likely to be associated with traumatic grief; de Vries et al. found subtle differences in responses to the death of a son or a daughter;

Hays et al. reported similarly fine differences in the contrast between a brother's death and a sister's death.

Such findings have broader implications in their allusions to variations in grievers, echoed in earlier discussions of potential personality, age, gender, ethnic/racial, and socio-economic status differences in bereavement. Such variations necessarily include contextual factors, including caregiving, institutionalization and other experiences of the final year of the deceased, as Moss et al. describe. Moreover, bereavement takes place in the context of prior loss experiences; just as there are differences between individuals in grief, so too are there differences within individuals—over time and across losses. This is an important point, particularly given an older population who have survived the deaths of many significant others. The lessons learned from these previous losses and the issues that remain to be resolved may once again gain prominence as individuals struggle with their grief. It is a noteworthy reminder that bereavement does not take place in an historical vacuum.

Nor does bereavement take place in a social vacuum. The bereft and those who surround him or her engage in an ongoing shaping of each other's experience. Fry's account of the grief of grandparents addresses this most directly. Recall that she identified as a factor in the process of bereavement the need to restructure relationships with family and other grandchildren. She also spoke of grandparents' suppression of grief so as not to add to the pain of their grieving adult children. Shaping of another type was introduced in Bower's examples of unresolved problems serving as barriers to acceptance; these included sibling conflicts and concurrent losses. Death and bereavement are family events [e.g., 4, 5, 22] and this network context is a necessary overlay if we are to fully understand the nature of reactions to loss.

The implications of these studies, however, are most directly and clearly presented in the article by Prigerson et al. The measure of traumatic grief they discuss, and its clear association with Post-Traumatic Stress Disorder, illustrates the origins, scope, and possible extent of bereavement reactions. Prigerson et al. target Cognitive Behavioral Therapy as an appropriate intervention strategy given its focus on the correction of distortions of thought and the enhancement of self-regulatory functioning. Therapeutic interventions with the bereft may direct their efforts toward the internal working models (or templates) of relationships that the bereft hold and assist in putting the deceased and their relationship with her or him in a more realistic light.

Along comparable lines, Bowers speaks of the heavily explained (i.e., much discussed) nature of death acceptance implicating the role of cultural expectations (including issues of timeliness of loss and courses of recovery) in the accounts of one's life. Fry discusses reminiscence and life review, shared with other grieving families and family members, as one of the ways in which bereft grandmothers attempted to reconcile their feelings and re-establish a sense of meaning in their lives. Hays et al. similarly mention the significance of shared life review between siblings in the context of what is lost with the death of a sibling. The importance and consequence of life review in the later years of life has been a frequently visited area of discussion in gerontology [see, for example, 49, 50]. Suggested herein is the potential of life review groups, perhaps structured to meet the special characteristics of the bereft, to assist in adaptation to bereavement.

One such group approach to life review has already been implicated in this respect. The Guided Autobiography [51-53] is a semi-structured, topical, group approach to life review. It entails a written component facilitating in-depth and personal reflection on the evocative themes of life and allowing participants to identify the threads that bind the fabric of the life story; it also entails a group experience which serves to enhance recall, reinforce participation and promote self-esteem. It has previously been suggested, and recalled here, that the Guided Autobiography may serve as an adjunct to bereavement self-help and support groups in that "individuals not only share in the recognition and grief surrounding the loss, but in the reconstruction of their lives given their loss" [53, p. 175]. It is an opportunity to develop new relationships and interpretations of the self, including the self as griever and timetables for "recovery."

ACKNOWLEDGMENTS

Thanks are due to Drs. John A. Blando, Joseph Mullan, and Linda Wardlaw for their helpful discussions and comments on an earlier version of this article.

REFERENCES

1. J. Bowlby, *Attachment and Loss: Volume 2. Separation: Anxiety and Anger*, Basic Books, New York, 1969.
2. D. A. Lund, Conclusions about Bereavement in Later Life and Implications for Interventions and Future Research, in *Older Bereaved Spouses: Research with Practical Applications*, D. A. Lund (ed.), Hemisphere, New York, pp. 215-231, 1989.
3. S. R. Schuchter and S. Zisook, The Course of Normal Grief, *Handbook of Bereavement: Theory, Research, and Intervention*, M. S. Stroebe, W. Stroebe, and R. O. Hansson (eds.), Cambridge University Press, New York, pp. 23-43, 1993.
4. B. de Vries, R. Dalla Lana, and V. Falck, Parental Bereavement over the Life Course: A Theoretical Intersection and Empirical Review, *Omega: Journal of Death and Dying*, 29:1, pp. 47-69, 1994.
5. M. McGoldbrick and F. Walsh, A Time to Mourn: Death and the Family Life Cycle, in *Living Beyond the Loss: Death in the Family*, F. Walsh and M. McGoldrick (eds.), W. W. Norton, New York, pp. 30-49, 1991.
6. M. A. Lieberman, All Family Losses are not Equal, *Journal of Family Psychology*, 2, pp. 368-372, 1989.
7. M. S. Stroebe, W. Stroebe, and R. O. Hansson, Bereavement Research: An Historical Introduction, *Journal of Social Issues*, 44:3, pp. 1-18, 1988.

8. C. B. Wortman and R. C. Silver, Coping with Irrevocable Loss, in *Cataclysms, Crises, and Catastrophes: Psychology in Action*, G. R. VandenBos and B. K. Bryant (eds.), American Psychological Association, Washington, pp. 189-235, 1987.
9. C. B. Wortman and R. C. Silver, The Myths of Coping with Loss, *Journal of Consulting and Clinical Psychology, 57*, pp. 349-357, 1989.
10. N. W. Arbuckle and B. de Vries, The Long-Term Effects of Later Life Spousal and Parental Bereavement on Personal Functioning, *The Gerontologist, 35*:4, pp. 637-647, 1995.
11. D. Kimmel, Psychotherapy and the Older Gay Man, *Psychotherapy: Theory, Research and Practice, 14*, pp. 386-393, 1977.
12. H. Z. Lopata, The Support Systems of American Urban Widows, in *Handbook of Bereavement: Theory, Research, and Intervention*, M. S. Stroebe, W. Stroebe, and R. O. Hansson (eds.), Cambridge University Press, New York, pp. 381-396, 1993.
13. D. Umberson, C. B. Wortman, and R. C. Kessler, Widowhood and Depression: Explaining Long-Term Gender Differences in Vulnerability, *Journal of Health and Social Behavior, 33*, pp. 10-24, 1992.
14. M. S. Moss and S. Z. Moss, The Death of a Parent, in *Midlife Loss: Coping Strategies*, R. Kalish (ed.), Sage, Newbury Park, California, pp. 89-114, 1989.
15. V. Marshall, *Last Chapters: A Sociology of Aging and Dying*, Brooks/Cole, Monterey, California, 1980.
16. G. O. Hagestad, The Continuous Bond: A Dynamic Multigenerational Perspective on Parent-Child Relations between Adults, in *Parent-Child Interactions and Parent-Child Relations in Child Development*, M. Perlmutter (ed.), Erlbaum, Hillsdale, New Jersey, pp. 129-158, 1984.
17. H. Anderson, The Death of a Parent: Its Impact on Middle-Aged Sons and Daughters, *Pastoral Psychology, 28*, pp. 151-167, 1980.
18. B. de Vries and V. T. Falck, *Interviews with Bereaved Parents*, unpublished data, University of Texas, School of Public Health, 1989.
19. J. Ponzetti, Bereaved Families: A Comparison of Parents' and Grandparents' Reactions to the Death of a Child, *Omega: Journal of Death and Dying, 25*, pp. 63-71, 1992.
20. J. Ponzetti and M. Johnson, The Forgotten Grievers: Grandparents' Reactions to the Death of Grandchildren, *Death Studies, 15*, pp. 157-167, 1991.
21. J. R. Averill and E. P. Nunley, Grief as an Emotion and as a Disease: A Social-Constructionist Perspective, in *Handbook of Bereavement: Theory, Research, and Intervention*, M. S. Stroebe, W. Stroebe, and R. O. Hansson (eds.), Cambridge University Press, New York, pp. 77-90, 1993.
22. P. C. Rosenblatt, Grief: The Social Context of Private Feelings, in *Handbook of Bereavement: Theory, Research, and Intervention*, M. S. Stroebe, W. Stroebe, and R. O. Hansson (eds.), Cambridge University Press, New York, pp. 102-111, 1993.
23. M. S. Stroebe, R. O. Hansson, and W. Stroebe, Contemporary Themes and Controversies in Bereavement Research, in *Handbook of Bereavement: Theory, Research, and Intervention*, M. S. Stroebe, W. Stroebe, and R. O. Hansson (eds.), Cambridge University Press, New York, pp. 457-475, 1993.
24. C. L. Johnson and L. E. Troll, Constraints and Facilitators to Friendships in Late Life, *The Gerontologist, 34*, pp. 79-87, 1994.

25. R. Kastenbaum, Death and Bereavement in Later Life, in *Death and Bereavement*, A. H. Kutscher (ed.), Charles C. Thomas, Springfield, Illinois, pp. 28-54, 1969.
26. T. A. Rando, The Unique Issues and Impact of the Death of a Child, in *Parental Loss of a Child*, T. A. Rando (ed.), Research Press, Champaign, Illinois, pp. 5-43, 1986.
27. B. L. Neugarten and K. K. Weinstein, The Changing American Grandparent, *Journal of Marriage and the Family, 26*, pp. 199-204, 1964.
28. D. T. Gold, Sibling Relationships in Old Age: A Typology, *International Journal of Aging and Human Development, 28*, pp. 37-51, 1989.
29. D. T. Gold, Late-Life Sibling Relationships: Does Race Affect Typological Distribution? *The Gerontologist, 30*, pp. 741-748, 1990.
30. D. T. Gold, M. A. Woodbury, and L. K. George, Relationship Classification Using Grade of Membership (GOM) Analysis: A Typology of Sibling Relationships in Later Life, *Journal of Gerontology, 45*, pp. 741-748, 1990.
31. W. Stroebe and M. S. Stroebe, *Bereavement and Health*, Cambridge University Press, New York, 1987.
32. D. R. Lehman, C. B. Wortman, and A. Williams, Long-Term Effects of Losing a Spouse or Child in a Motor Vehicle Crash, *Journal of Personality and Social Psychology, 52*:1, pp. 218-231, 1987.
33. R. S. Weiss, Loss and Recovery, in *Handbook of Bereavement: Theory, Research, and Intervention*, M. S. Stroebe, W. Stroebe, and R. O. Hansson (eds.), Cambridge University Press, New York, pp. 271-284, 1993.
34. G. Gorer, *Death, Grief and Mourning*, Doubleday, Garden City, New York, 1965.
35. M. Osterweis, F. Solomon, and M. Green, *Bereavement: Reactions, Consequences and Care*, National Academy Press, Washington, D.C., 1984.
36. M. S. Caserta and D. Lund, Bereavement Stress and Coping among Older Adults: Expectations versus the Actual Experience, *Omega: Journal of Death and Dying, 25*:1, pp. 33-45, 1992.
37. R. Kastenbaum, Dying and Death: A Life-Span Approach, in *Handbook of the Psychology of Aging* (2nd Edition), J. E. Birren and K. W. Schaie (eds.), Van Nostrand Reinhold, New York, pp. 619-643, 1985.
38. P. C. Rosenblatt, *Bitter, Bitter Tears: Nineteenth Century Diarists and Twentieth Century Grief Theories*, University of Minnesota Press, Minneapolis, Minnesota, 1983.
39. B. de Vries, C. Jacoby, and C. G. Davis, Ethnic Differences in Later Life Friendship, *Canadian Journal on Aging, 15*:2, pp. 226-244, 1996.
40. E. S. Deck and J. R. Folta, The Friend-Griever, in *Disenfranchised Grief: Recognizing Hidden Sorrow*, K. J. Doka (ed.), Lexington Books, Lexington, Massachusetts, pp. 77-89, 1989.
41. B. de Vries, The Understanding of Friendship: An Adult Life Course Perspective, in *Handbook of Emotion, Adult Development, and Aging*, C. Malatesta-Magai and S. J. McFadden (eds.), Academic Press, New York, pp. 249-268, 1996.
42. C. B. Wortman, R. C. Silver, and R. C. Kessler, The Meaning of Loss and Adjustment to Bereavement, in *Handbook of Bereavement: Theory, Research, and Intervention*, M. S. Stroebe, W. Stroebe, and R. O. Hansson (eds.), Cambridge University Press, New York, pp. 349-366, 1993.

43. R. S. Lazarus and S. Folkman, *Stress, Appraisal, and Coping*, Springer, New York, 1984.
44. J. B. Miller, *Toward a New Psychology of Women*, Beacon Press, Boston, Massachusetts, 1976.
45. S. Parker and B. de Vries, Patterns of Friendship for Women and Men in Same and Cross-Sex Relationships, *Journal of Social and Personal Relationships, 10*, pp. 617-626, 1993.
46. P. H. Wright, Interpreting Research on Gender Differences in Friendship: A Case for Moderation and a Plea for Caution, *Journal of Social and Personal Relationships, 5*, pp. 367-373, 1988.
47. W. C. Fish, Differences of Grief Intensity in Bereaved Parents, in *Parental Loss of a Child*, T. A. Rando (ed.), Research Press, Chicago, Illinois, pp. 415-430, 1986.
48. B. Shanfield and B. J. Swain, Death of Adult Children in Traffic Accidents, *Journal of Nervous and Mental Disease, 172*, pp. 533-538, 1984.
49. B. K. Haight, Reminiscing: The State of the Art as a Basis for Practice, *International Journal of Aging and Human Development, 33*, pp. 1-32, 1991.
50. B. K. Haight and S. Hendrix, An Integrated Review of Reminiscence, in *The Art and Science of Reminiscing: Theory, Research, Methods, and Applications*, B. K. Haight and J. D. Webster (eds.), Taylor and Francis, Washington, D.C., pp. 3-21, 1995.
51. J. E. Birren and D. E. Deutchman, *Guiding Autobiography Groups for Older Adults: Exploring the Fabric of Life*, Johns Hopkins University Press, Baltimore, Maryland, 1991.
52. B. de Vries, J. E. Birren, and D. E. Deutchman, Adult Development through Guided Autobiography: The Family Context, *Family Relations, 39*, pp. 3-7, 1990.
53. B. de Vries, J. E. Birren, and D. E. Deutchman, Method and Uses of the Guided Autobiography, in *The Art and Science of Reminiscing: Theory, Research, Methods, and Applications*, B. K. Haight and J. D. Webster (eds.), Taylor and Francis, Washington, D.C., pp. 165-177, 1995.